PARADISE IS FULL OF BUGS

PARADISE
IS FULL
OF BUGS

W. A. Corley

BLUE HERON BOOKS 1997

Published by
Blue Heron Books
9697 Sicard Flat Rd.
Browns Valley, CA 95918

ISBN: 0-9656099-0-1

Library of Congress Cataloging-in-Publication Data

Corley, W.A., 1929–
    Paradise is full of bugs / W.A. Corley.
        p.   cm.
    ISBN 0-9656099-0-1
    1. Corley, W.A., 1929–   —journeys.   2. Evenin Star (ketch).
3. Voyages and travels.   4. Shipwrecks—Micronesia (Federated
States)—Ponape.   5. Pacific Ocean.   I. Title.
C477.C78 1997
910.4'5—dc21   97-5007
                                                                          CIP

Back cover photo by Patricia Silva

Printed in the United States of America

10   9   8   7   6   5   4   3   2   1

TABLE OF CONTENTS

PREFACE

Before satellite navigation and fiberglass boat construction, the vast stretches of the Pacific saw very few small boat sailors. For fifty years after the great age of sail and when whalers ceased to roam the oceans, only an occasional wooden sailing vessel would venture into the South Seas. Island cultures were more or less undisturbed. To make a Pacific voyage in those days was to truly be on your own with almost no contact with the outside world. It was for loners and people who loved solitude and the simple, no-frills, existence of life at sea.

When "Evening Star" set sail on the odyssey described in this book, her skipper didn't realize that he was experiencing the end of an era. Within a few years, the age of fiberglass boats and electronic navigation would allow hundreds of small boats to venture onto the oceans of the world. The old, timeless skills of celestial navigation, marlinspike seamanship and the maintenance problems of wooden sailing vessels would no longer be a prerequisite for offshore sailing. Modern technology would provide many gadgets and devices to circumvent older, hard learned skills. Long-range communications now keep the small boat sailor in constant touch with the outside world and provide a means of chatting with others on a daily basis at sea for information and companionship. This eliminates the fear of facing the sea and elements totally alone.

Change is inevitable. Quiet anchorages are now filled with a new breed of sailor who has taken all the modern conveniences of a shoreside home with him, and the main activity in the island ports seems to be a social thing. I believe the loners who sailed the Pacific for so many years are now a dying breed and, I confess, I was one of them.

PROLOGUE

THE RAIN DRIVES IN HORIZONTALLY from the starboard quarter hurled by the freshening northeast tradewinds of the Western Pacific. It sets up one hell of a noise as it pelts the oilskins of the lone figure hunched over the wheel. The ship runs free but needs a little help. It has been a night of squalls and shifting wind conditions, and the man is tired from adjusting sails and altering the steering vane frequently. Between trips to the deck he has slipped below and crawled into the charthouse bunk for catnaps until some slight change in the wind or noise from the rigging brings him instantly awake again.

It is almost over. The first light of the approaching dawn will be along soon. He thinks of the sleeping girls; one in the leeward bunk of the main cabin and the other up forward. It makes him feel good knowing they are deep into a comfortable night's rest and he hasn't had to disturb them. This has been the custom for many month's of sailing. They stay awake during the early hours of the evening while he gets some sleep after dinner. Then he, along with the wind steering vane, takes it the rest of the night. Most of the time, this is a good arrangement. Only on nights such as this is it a bit exhausting with little chance for rest.

He is weary when the vane, now adjusted for an acceptable course, engages the wheel and seems to accept control again. The rain stings his face as he straightens up and squints hard to take a look across the foredeck into the black wet night. Visibility is zero and he sees nothing. His glance is automatically to starboard because that is where the big high island of Ponape should be somewhere in the darkness ahead. He must be heading for a point south of the island because the frequent changes of course have all been southerly through the night. Had he not been so tired he might also have remembered there was a strong north flowing current to be encountered as the ship approaches the island. For now, he contents himself that there will be plenty of time to get a position in the morning and hopefully, find a good anchorage before another nightfall. It has been only four days since leaving the island of Kusie, but in this weather that's quite enough.

With a final glance at the compass and the big squaresail set and drawing, he steps quickly through the hatch and into the warmth of the chartroom. A puddle of water forms around his bare feet as he slips out of the rain gear and shoves it under the ladder. For a moment he thinks of waking Susie for a watch and going to bed himself, but the thought of disturbing her from a sound warm sleep on a night like this always bothers him. He is still a father first and the skipper second. What the hell—hang on for a while longer, until daybreak anyway. In the meantime, maybe a cup of hot tea will revive him.—The ship's clock chimes the half hour. It is 0430 in the morning.

The rush of fast water and unusual motion of the boat brings him instantly awake and on his feet. With a sick dread in the pit of his stomach, he knows even before he reaches the hatch, the vessel is on a reef. He charges onto the deck and grabs the mizzen halyard for support as the boat grinds to a halt, careens slightly and settles into a fifteen degree list to port.

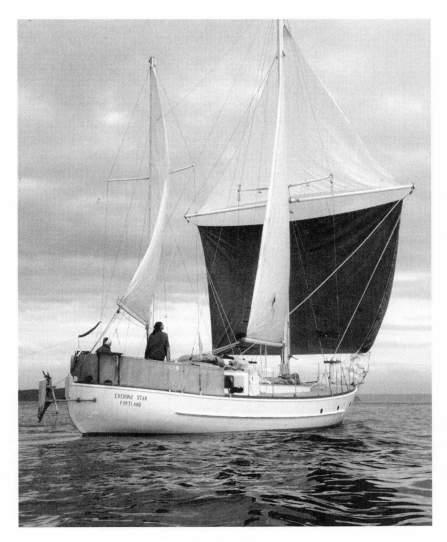

Evening Star

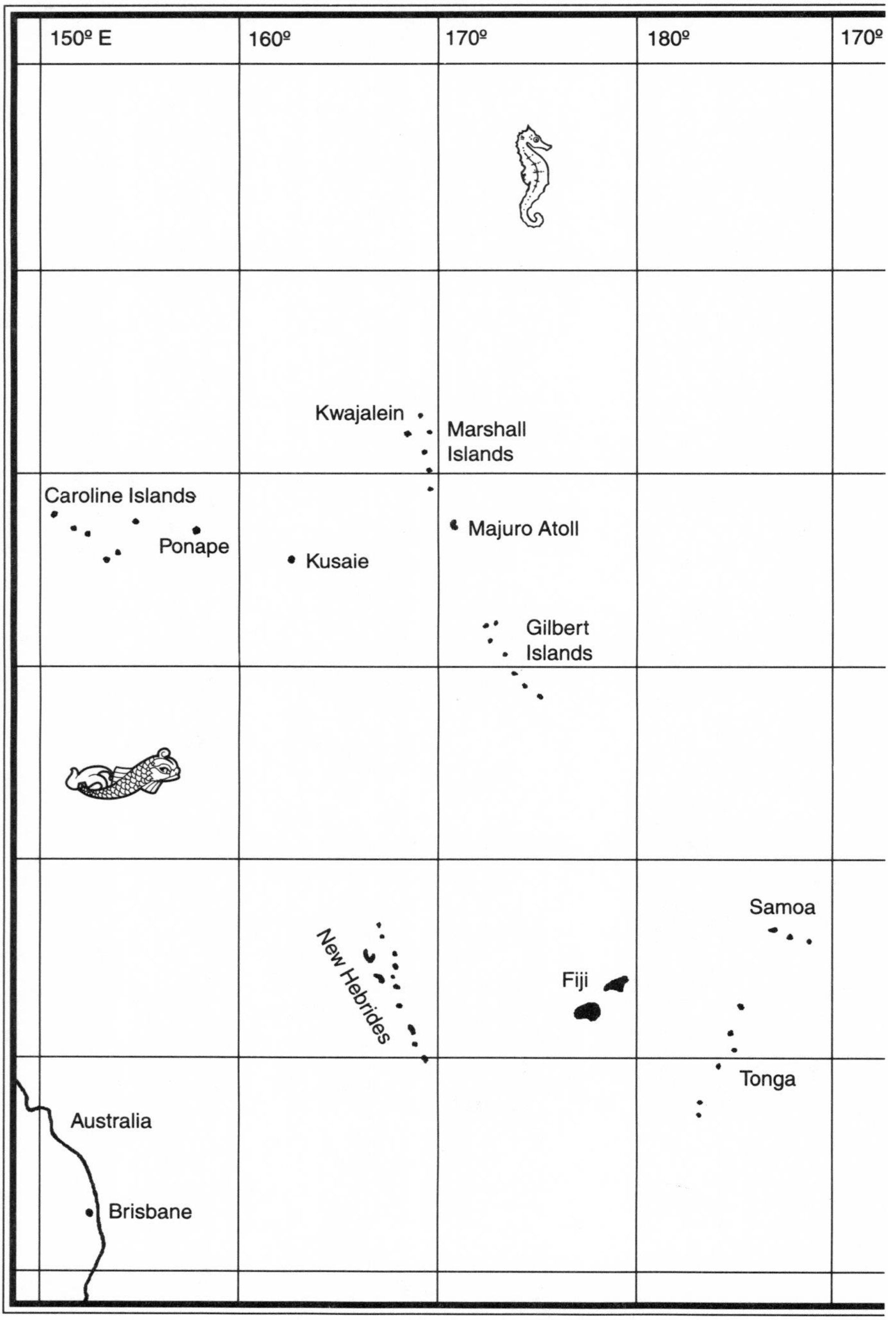

150º E	160º	170º	180º	170º

Kwajalein
Marshall
Islands

Caroline Islands
Ponape
Majuro Atoll
Kusaie

Gilbert
Islands

New Hebrides

Samoa

Fiji

Tonga

Australia

Brisbane

Western Pacific Islands

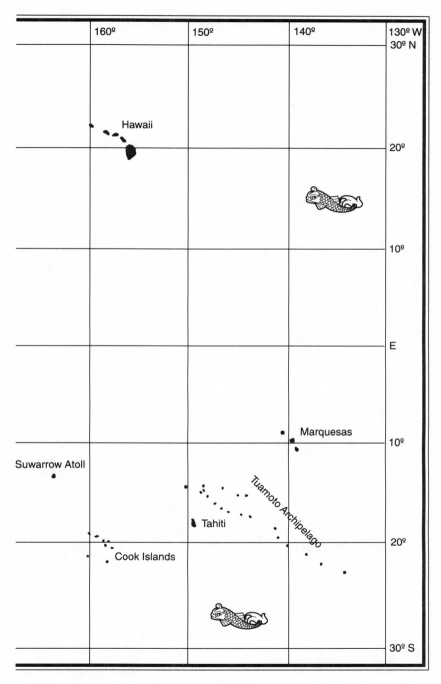

Central Pacific Islands

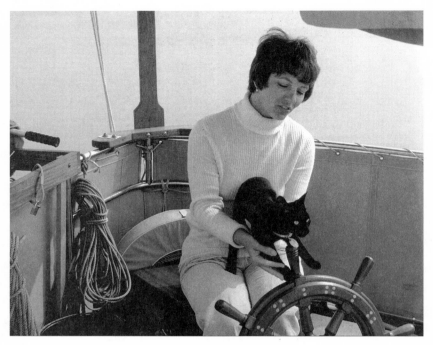

Jeanne at helm with cat

The Skipper

PART ONE

The Dream

CHAPTER ONE

THE DREAM OF ADVENTURING in a small sailing ship was nurtured many years ago, but the first positive step came in the late sixties. The recall is clear. I stepped out of a rented car and headed for a sleek little aircraft on the transient flightline.

Bonanza 9827 Romeo—This is Boeing Tower. You are cleared for takeoff. Instinctively, I eased the plane out onto the center of the runway and applied full power.

It was September 23, 1969, and I felt buoyed and elated as the plane lifted easily into the Seattle morning air and started it's climb southward to 10,000 feet. The scenery in this area is breathtaking on those rare days when the sun finds it's way through the overcast and I drank it in. At 10,500 feet I levelled off and did my work. Throttle back to 2300 RPM. Manifold pressure back to 23 inches. Lean the mixture a tad more and trim for level flight. With the nose down just a hair, she roared southward. What a great feeling. Three thousand hours of that kind of travel and I still enjoyed the sensation of flying an airplane. It was time to set the radio frequency to the first of a string of beacon stations that would guide me in steps to California but, somehow, that would have ruined the feeling. I banked the plane slowly to the right and headed southwest for the Oregon coast.

A sense of freedom engulfed me as I thought about the far reaching effects of the simple decision I had made and expressed to my business associates only hours before. Why does a man decide to give up the comfort, security, prestige and monetary rewards of the corporate existence to pursue a simpler life? I was not sure I knew. At 40 years of age, I was deeply entrenched in the corporate structure of a progressive company and already well up the income ladder. The challenging responsibilities and earnings from being at the top of my profession were just ahead. What then was this thing pulling me away from what most men were reaching for, and hoping for, with every fibre of their being? Maybe my sense of values was distorted. All I knew was that I had always followed my instincts and at this moment they told me I had just paved the way for a much more meaningful existence.

The early winter sun was beginning to move lower across the sky in these higher latitudes and it felt warm as it poured through the plexiglass in front of me. For an instant, the coffee steamed the side window as I poured half a cup.

If I was to make this dream of sailing the oceans of the world a reality, I would need a ship, money and a plan. At that moment I had only one of the three: a thirteen ton sailing ketch tied up in Oxnard, California. With it, was my wife and a mortgage. The woman was an asset. Good companion, good sailor and willing to share adventures. The mortgage was the symbol of my financial situation. Definitely a liability. Then, there was the responsibility of being a father. My oldest daughter was almost ready to enter college, my fourteen year old son was having teenage problems and was reluctant to stay in junior high school, and a little girl of eight would need all the love and help she could get while growing up. Obviously, adventuring for me would have to wait for awhile, but the decision had been irrevocably made.

The magnitude of all these obstacles was too much for my impractical mind at the moment and, lest they dampen my ignorant reverie, I turned my attention to the incoming tide race as it forced it's way against the current of the mighty Columbia river. Off to my right the Pacific stretched on to an endless unbroken horizon. I could already feel the beautiful loneliness of the Oregon coast and I gave in to the urge to be closer to it. A slight pressure on the wheel and the plane dropped lower. The airspeed climbed toward a thin red line on the instrument panel and I throttled back and descended to 5500 feet.

How many years had it been since I first started thinking about sailing the oceans of the world in a small boat? I guess it went all the way back to 1949 when I was flying the Pacific as a radio operator aboard Navy transport planes. During my two and a half years in the Pacific I acquired a taste for warm weather and salt water and it had never left me. After my tour in the Navy, the long road toward financial stability, and hopefully independence, was begun. It seemed a pretty slow road for a young man without a college education and not the slightest notion of where to begin. To accomplish something financially was one of my first major goals and I viewed it as not only the road to adventure but an adventure in itself.

In the beginning, it seemed like an impossible task as I tried to support a young family on $70.00 a week while always holding down two jobs or going to school at night. I had faith in the system though, and complete faith in myself, so I continued to work and to dream. It was challenging and enjoyable. An early decision was to leave my native Texas environment and move to the west coast to be close to the ocean and boats. I moved to Newport Beach, California and soon had employment in a shipyard. Those were exciting days, sitting on the docks during lunch break and watching the fish in clear water with seagoing activity all around. I was in my element.

Secondary jobs included everything. I fry-cooked in a drive-in restaurant. I was a janitor and cleaned two Bank of America buildings each night. I cleaned charter-fishing boats and had many other odd jobs. Primary jobs changed from the shipyard to a selling job in San Francisco, servicing radar at an aircraft plant in the desert, sales manager for a wholesale electronics firm in Santa Ana and, finally, a business for myself in a television and appliance store back in Newport Beach. By this time, I was thirty years old and had purchased my first sailing boat, a twenty-four foot heavy-displacement cruising sloop. She wasn't much of a boat, but I sailed her frequently in all kinds of weather. I had also managed to accumulate almost three years of college credits by going to school at night. The next step was to find a progressive, young company that was growing and might provide a vehicle to greater earnings. I found just that in a mortgage insurance company and joined their field sales organization in 1959.

I didn't care much for selling insurance but I was excited about the company, it's people and it's growth possibilities. That was enough for me and I rose through the ranks and a succession of management jobs. It was at this point in my career that I told my friend and boss, as well as a new company president, that I intended to go to sea as soon as possible instead of pursuing the American dream any further. Even though I had been successful to a certain degree, I was determined not to become entrapped in the system to the point where dreams of adventurous undertakings were out of the question. It was one of the easiest decisions of my life and, at the same time, one of the toughest.

The lights of Santa Barbara began to appear as I glided across the sharp mountain range behind the city at dusk. The smoky outline of Santa Cruz Island lying thirty miles off the coast seemed peaceful and inviting in the last light of the already downed sun. The past became the present as I eased back on the throttle and lowered the nose for the final descent to home. At a thousand feet over the wide sand beach five miles north of Oxnard Harbor, I leveled off and allowed the airspeed of over 200 miles an hour to drop as I lined up for the cluster of boats lying quietly at their berths. I roared over the marina at 200 feet and flashed the landing lights at a familiar little ship among the nesting boats. Then a climbing turn, and it was almost done.

Ventura County tower—This is Bonanza 9827 Romeo— I'm over the power plant for landing. — A short interval and I was not alone anymore as the radio came alive.—Bonanza 9827 Romeo—This is Ventura County tower. You are cleared to land runway 26. The wind is calm. The altimeter is Two Niner Eight Five.—Report right downwind.—Is Ventura County your final destination? —Over.

I was tempted to tell him—It's only the beginning.

CHAPTER TWO

THIS LIFELONG SAILING DREAM OF MINE would probably have been made with or without a soulmate, but with the one I had, it was made successfully and with the greatest enjoyment.

Jeanne was a special person.

We met in Phoenix at a party given for the apartment complex we both lived in. When introduced, I was immediately attracted not only to the beautiful young girl of twenty-eight, but to a warm, outgoing personality that was a magnet to anyone she met. We started dating and, of course, she learned of my dream to sail the oceans of the world. On the surface, it seemed she was an unlikely candidate to share in such a dream.

She was born and raised in San Antonio, Texas of a fairly well to do family, and had led a typical sheltered and easy life. Considering the adventures she eventually shared with me, it seems funny that she could not even own a bicycle as a child because her parents thought it too dangerous to be riding the streets of the neighborhood. She was married briefly to the son of the Mayor. After the divorce, she moved to Phoenix to be on her own and start a new life. When we met she had a job as a service representative with the telephone company and was making her own way.

I was the Arizona sales manager for my insurance company and just beginning to move up in management and income. We were both young, restless and eager to experience new things. I had all the tools to accomplish that desire. I flew a small private plane in pursuit of my business around the state and had recently replaced my first boat with a beautiful little Tahiti Ketch called "El Viento." The boat was berthed in San Diego and I flew over to sail her almost every weekend. Jeanne was soon accompanying me on these excursions and proved to be an able and enthusiastic sailor.

This idyllic existence was interrupted some months later when I was given a new and more important job of trouble-shooting in other areas of the country. My first assignment took me to Kansas City and I was away a lot for awhile. Sometime later, I was sent on another mission to Milwaukee which looked like it might be a long assignment. I missed Jeanne terribly and knew there was only one way to solve this problem. I was divorced with three children and was, frankly, scared of the thought of marriage, but threw caution to the wind and proposed. She accepted and we went before a judge in Phoenix on September 1, 1966.

Jeanne quit her job, and our life became one of constant travel the next several years. Together we established operations for the company all over the United States from Minnesota to Florida to Texas. She took care of me while I interviewed and trained people at every post I was sent to. What could have been a very tiring job became a real pleasure as we travelled the country and worked. We were constant companions in everything. It was not all work. We took side trips to the Bahama Islands when we were in that area, and dove off the reefs in the Florida Keys. As we passed through Texas on our trips we would stop for visits with either her parents in San

Antonio, or mine in Dallas. I think her folks finally accepted me, adventurous spirit and all, and knew I made her happy. I sure enjoyed, and learned to love, them both. My own parents thought Jeanne was the ultimate in womanhood, and I realized they were right.

All the work was a means to an end for us. She now shared my dream of adventuring in small boats and we made plans to do it when we were financially able. When we were not travelling, every minute was spent aboard "El Viento" off the California coast and we sailed the boat and explored the Channel Islands. We loved the quiet anchorages and wildlife, and it was good preparation for the big adventure we were planning. Jeanne was an excellent cook and was very capable as first mate aboard the boat. Because of the nature of my job our home base could be anywhere, and we moved to suit our pleasure. We moved from San Diego to the Channel Islands Marina in Oxnard, then to Berkeley, and finally to Seattle. While in Oxnard, we rented a beautiful little apartment overlooking our berth but, after awhile, it was obvious we spent very little time there. When we were home from a work trip, we climbed aboard the boat and headed for the islands. It was then that we finally broke the ties of land and moved permanently aboard our little vessel.

El Viento was a beautifully built Tahiti Ketch which I had now owned for eight years. Her design had taken many people around the world in the past and we loved just being aboard. She was only thirty-one feet long with a ten-foot beam, but Jeanne made her a pleasant home. While all of our peers and contemporaries were building and living in beautiful shoreside homes, we were quite content with our lives and envied none of them. Once we moved aboard, we never looked back. It was the first step toward our planned adventure and we were happy as clams. Everyone we knew could never understand how any woman could live in such cramped quarters and like it. They were in awe of her and of my good fortune in having such a mate. I don't know of anyone who didn't enjoy an evening aboard with the warmth and good food that Jeanne served in abundance on both counts. We laughed at their skepticism of our lifestyle and actually felt sorry for them that they could not know the pleasures we had.

It was to be over three more years before the first voyage of our planned adventure began, but they were productive ones and provided us with a larger vessel and the financial base I needed. Once I had a plan firmly in mind I called Grant and requested a meeting. He was my boss and trusted friend of many years. It was through his guidance that I had grown in the business and in the company. We met for lunch in the Washington Plaza Hotel in Seattle and I knew he was wondering what this meeting was all about. When our order was taken and the waitress moved away, I stated my mission forthrightly.

"I want the job of National Director of Sales. I've thought a great deal about it and I believe the company needs my services here in Seattle. It goes without saying, I know I can do a good job for you."

I knew I had been considered for this job for some time although it had never been offered or even mentioned directly. The problem, of course, was my stated decision to leave at some time in the near future. After only a brief pause, Grant responded.

"This is one of the better days of my life if you're serious, Bill, but what about your plans to sail the Pacific?"

"To be honest with you, those plans haven't changed, but I am not financially able to make the break yet. In the meantime, the company has been in a no-growth situation for five years and a new office building is already in the planning stage. I know we have also expended a bundle of capitol for the new computer system in anticipation of growth. Frankly, I am somewhat concerned about the future of the company. There are too many good people, many of them hired and trained by me, who have worked hard to build a future for themselves and

I don't want anything to diminish that possibility. Because of my work in the field, there isn't anyone who knows the problems of the field organization better than I do. I honestly believe I can do something about getting us back into a growth posture again and I am willing to commit enough time to get the job done."

I anticipated his next question. "What kind of time frame are you thinking about, Bill."

"Frankly, I'm thinking in terms of three years."

That afternoon, after a brief conference with the President and Chairman of the Board, I was given the job of National Director of Sales and agreed to move immediately to Seattle to begin my new task. Within a week Jeanne and I sailed "El Viento" from California for a new anchorage on Puget Sound and one of the greatest business challenges of my life.

CHAPTER THREE

WE ARRIVED IN PUGET SOUND at the end of the season. Fall soon turned into winter and we had a berth in the little town of Kingston on the Olympic Peninsula. The boat harbor was adjacent to the Kingston Ferry dock and I commuted to work on it. There was snow on the docks some mornings and I left a single pair of tracks as I walked to catch the early morning ferry to work. I enjoyed the ride across the sound to Edmonds each day and usually had breakfast from the snack bar on the way. Steam heat fogged the windows of the little ship and a walk outside on the decks was a great bracer to start the day. Seattle is a real marine town and the sights and sounds along with the smell of salt air quickens the pulse of any sailor. I was no exception.

The second year of our stay in Washington, my financial situation improved and I was shopping around for a larger vessel. On a visit to see family in Northern California at Christmas, I found what I was looking for. An ad in a sailing magazine caught my attention and I flew to Newport Beach to check out a forty-two foot boat called "Evening Star."

She was a ruggedly-built wooden ketch, designed by Hugh Angleman and built by Willard Boat Works in Costa Mesa. Her beam was fourteen feet. She carried 350 gallons of diesel fuel, 200 gallons of water, and fully- loaded, displaced about twenty-five tons. She was a very strongly built little ship, of mahogany and oak, and my first impression of her was solid muscle, exactly what I wanted.

The accommodations below decks were spacious and broken up into three cabins. The chartroom, aft, was raised enough to have a full view of the decks, and with a comfortable table and dinette, provided a perfect place to take our meals as well as watch the world go by. An opening between the chartroom and galley made it easy to pass food through as well as provide a pleasant contact with the cook while she prepared the evening meals.

The galley was as complete and spacious as a small apartment kitchen and had all the conveniences: propane gas stove and oven, pressure water system, refrigeration and plenty of work space. Before leaving for the Pacific, I would eliminate the refrigeration and install manual hand pumps for both fresh and salt water. At sea, refrigeration takes a lot of electrical power to keep running, and after a few days there is no more

fresh food to keep cold anyway. With manual pumps and not much need for electricity, we could sail for weeks without having to run the engine.

The main salon was also the master stateroom. It had a full-size double berth and another table and dinette area opposite with plenty of storage space and bookshelves all around. At the head of this spacious cabin and built into a bulkhead was a beautiful little wood burning fireplace. Forward of the main cabin was the "head" with a great full- sized shower and past that, the forward cabin with two more berths and a work-table opposite. Forward of this private little cabin was the peak which contained the chain and sail locker. An eighty-five horsepower Perkins diesel engine provided auxiliary power to push us about six knots in smooth sea conditions. I spent a day going through her from stem to stern and made an offer before flying back to Seattle. Within a month she was ours, and I made arrangements to take leave from the company for a few weeks and sail her to Seattle via the Hawaiian Islands.

We sailed in April for Hawaii with my mother and dad, then in their sixties, as crew to help Jeanne and me. Sixteen days out of Newport Beach we raised the island of Maui to complete our first long ocean passage. After a month back in Seattle to catch up on my business activities, I flew back to Hawaii and sailed her on to Seattle. Our crew on that leg of the voyage was Ken Murray, a long time friend. We made the passage to Puget Sound in nineteen days. On this five thousand mile ocean voyage I learned a lot about our vessel, about my capabilities, and most importantly, about the sea itself which was to be our road to adventure and sometimes our adversary in the years to come.

A few months later, El Viento was sold to a professional seaman and we sailed along with her for some miles up Puget Sound as she departed for other waters and unknown adventures. Jeanne and I hated to see her sail over the horizon and out of our lives. She was a special ship and we loved her.

The job with the company took three years. I buried myself in it at the beginning and didn't come up for air for eighteen months. At the end of that time we had completely reorganized a field sales force and changed it from an entrepreneurial-type operation to a corporate-team concept. The results were dramatic and impressive. The first year, we had growth of a modest ten percent. The second year we soared to thirty percent. I was well compensated for my work and given appropriate recognition for my contributions. It was heady, exhilarating and exhausting, and it almost aborted my sailing plans.

The docks were quiet on a blustery March day as I parked as close to "G" dock as possible. I reached into the back seat of my old convertible for a propane bottle and backed out with the awkward load. The twinge in my back was not severe as I put the bottle down and straightened up a moment to relieve it then moved off down the dock toward the boat. I didn't realize it at the moment, but it was the beginning of an ordeal.

The slight nagging pain in my lower back didn't go away during the next few days. Instead, it became worse. I tried every kind of exercise to relieve it but soon it was keeping me from sleeping at night. The pain reached alarming proportions two weeks later when I tried to get into my car one morning, so I asked Jeanne to drive me to the office. The full realization that something was terribly wrong came when she stopped in front of the office and I tried to get out of the car. The pain was intense and I could not manage it without a real struggle. I simply said, "let's go home." That was the last time I worked for six weeks.

I have never been one for patronizing doctors, but things became worse. Finally the decision to see one was made for me by a friend at the office. He was on the Board of Directors of a local hospital and knew a good back specialist there. He arranged for me to see this doctor and, with the help of another friend who had a panel truck, loaded me into the back like a side of beef and drove me to the hospital. I felt defeated. I went

14

in with the only pair of pajamas I owned, a shaving kit, a small disguised bottle of brandy, and a nagging fear that my strength of body was gone. It was truly one of the low points in my life. I felt completely out of control.

After a week of traction which didn't help, I came face to face with the doctor and the inevitable. He didn't try to sell me anything but just laid the facts on the table. I had a ruptured disk in the last vertebrae in my back and it was pinching the sciatic nerve, partially paralyzing my leg. It was something that could be fixed with an operation but with a small risk of permanent damage. I sent Jeanne to the university medical book store for a copy of *Grey's Anatomy* and then had another session with the doctor. He carefully explained the procedure using the pictures and diagrams in the newest addition to our medical library and I said, "let's do it."

My first sailing date was now only a few months away. I had a lot at stake. The company had been given notice that I would leave at the end of the year and they were already looking for a replacement to be brought aboard, hopefully, six months before I departed. In order to leave by year's end I needed to sail the boat south to California before the northern winter set in. While I was lying incapacitated on my boat prior to entering the hospital, Grant asked me if I didn't want to look at my hole card and reconsider before they reached a hiring decision on a replacement. I said "no."

Half drugged, you lie on a roll-around table in an empty hall outside the operating room and wait your turn. When it comes, they roll you in, make a little small talk, give you an injection that wells up as a strong sensation in your throat, and it's good-by faces, lights and reality.

The operation was on a Friday night, and by Saturday morning I couldn't move any part of my body without intense pain. It was more frightening than before the operation. I was anxious to try to move and by Sunday, with the help of several nurses to hold everything in place, I was helped out of bed and on my feet. To my great embarrassment, I almost immediately passed out and was put back to bed. That was the low point though, and after that, the strength came back fast. With the aid of a therapist I was on my feet within the next twenty-four hours.

On Monday I asked the doctor if I could go home to recuperate rather than stay in the hospital. He said I could leave anytime I was able to walk out under my own power. On Tuesday morning I took a test run down the hall and made it to the nurse's station and back. I was totally exhausted but called Jeanne and asked her to come and get me as soon as possible. There was a big ebb tide that morning and once it was well underway, I wouldn't be able to make it down the steep dock ramp. That afternoon, four days after the operation, I was sitting on the deck of my boat in sunshine, and the fear of defeat was gone.

The last half of 1973 was a time of national turmoil. The sickening tragedy of Viet Nam was being felt by all, and the Watergate fiasco was constantly in the news. My job with the company was essentially over and I had accomplished what I set out to do three years earlier. My replacement had already been hired and he, naturally, had his own ideas of what the company direction should be from that point on. To more or less get me out of the way, I was allowed to move myself and the boat to Southern California in preparation for the voyage before the northern winter set in. Although I was officially still in charge, it was a lame- duck situation for me. I was exhausted with the corporate effort and, needless to say, was happy to abdicate in favor of a warmer clime and to get out of the pressure cooker of corporate affairs. My mind was now on the upcoming voyage and the vast reaches of the Pacific.

I had only one nagging fear: Was I strong enough to take "Evening Star" to sea after only a few months out of back surgery? I felt great and ready to find out.

CHAPTER FOUR

IN THE LATE AFTERNOON of August 3, 1973, fully loaded with fuel, water and groceries, "Evening Star" nosed her fat snout into Puget Sound and headed out on the first leg of her trip to Southern California. The captain and crew, consisting of Jeanne, my daughter, Susie, and my mother and dad, were all in high spirits. My parents had flown to Seattle to work as crew on the trip down the coast. It was all sunshine and warm weather as we sailed up the sound headed for Admiralty Inlet and the eastern end of the Strait of Juan de Fuca. By early evening we were approaching Admiralty Inlet and the winds had raised a strong head-sea making it difficult to make headway under power. We decided it would be easier going in the morning, so we bore off to Port Townsend to spend the night in a pleasant anchorage.

The following morning we had no difficulty powering around the inlet in light fog, but picked up a strong head-wind and seas again by noon. It was very uncomfortable for all hands, but especially so for my mother and dad. Consequently, I put into Port Angeles before dinnertime for another quiet anchorage. Over dinner my dad had to tell me that he and Mother didn't feel they were quite up to the trip if it should remain rough and that they had decided to abandon the trip and return home. I was disappointed, of course, but certainly understood as they were both in their late sixties. They left in the morning of the following day, and the rest of us decided to wait until evening before resuming our trip in the hope of finding less wind and head-seas during the evening hours. Our assumption was correct, and by midmorning of the following day we were finally at the broad entrance to the Strait of Juan de Fuca and able to lay off the wind enough to raise all sail and shape a course to round Cape Flattery.

After three days of head-winds and rough chop it was a welcome relief to be under sail, but that proved to be short lived. In trying to take another turn or two on the main halyard winch I found the halyard to be jammed in the shieve at the top of the mainmast. This posed a dilemma. I either had to backtrack to the quiet water of Neah Bay for repairs or try to get up there and fix it. After the difficult three days we had already experienced trying to get to sea I was in no mood to turn around, so we maneuvered the boat in the long Pacific swells to get the least roll and prepared a bosun's chair to get me up to the problem.

If you've never experienced trying to climb a mast in the open sea, you can't imagine the difficulty involved. It takes a lot of strength to keep from being wrenched from the mast as the boat rolls, so you have to hold on while trying to work at the same time. Freeing the halyard was not a problem, but getting to it required taking six screws out of a shield in front of it. That simple job took fifteen minutes. As I hung on for dear life fifty feet off the water and worked at that tedious chore, I was painfully aware that this was a major test of my strength only four months out of back surgery. When the girls lowered me to the deck after the repair was completed I was totally exhausted and for awhile, I could hardly move. My crew took over for the rest of the day, and under full sail again we headed south, free of the land, and I was a little more sure of my ability and strength to handle any physical test from here on.

For six days we sailed down the coast of Washington, Oregon and California in rain and cloudy weather with winds sometimes reaching thirty knots. It was not the most pleasant weather, especially for August, but we were finally free of work commitments and headed south to warmer climes anticipating new experiences in the coming months. Early one afternoon we rounded Point Reyes in the sunshine and laid a course down the Marin headlands for the Golden Gate. By early evening we entered San Francisco Bay and found an empty slip at the St. Francis Yacht Club under the city.

For a full three days we relaxed and played tourist around the waterfront and provisioned the boat for our next leg to Southern California. Then, on August 16th, we passed again under the Golden Gate, early in the morning, and headed south. Two days later, late in the afternoon, we sailed past the big rock sentinels guarding Cuyler Harbor on San Miguel Island and anchored under the cliffs. This is an island that is not often visited. Geographically located off Point Conception and the northernmost of the Channel Islands, it has a different climate than the islands only a few miles south. Even though this was late summer, we experienced mostly cool, cloudy and windy weather since leaving Seattle and San Miguel was no exception. We spent a cool, windy night at anchor before moving on early the next morning. By afternoon we found what we were looking for. Johnson's Lee, an anchorage on the outside of Santa Rosa Island, was a beautiful spot with kelp beds and clear water, and when the anchor went down the heavy clothes came off and it was hot.

Point Conception, about fifty miles north of Santa Barbara, is a distinctive weather dividing line. The marine weather north of that line is more or less the same all the way to Alaska. Colder, wetter and stronger winds, and bigger seas are the norm, while south of that line, all the way to it's counterpart somewhere off the coast of Chili, just the opposite is true. We were happy to be on the warm side of that line and we soaked up the sun and solitude at Johnson's Lee for three days before moving on. Our next stop was little Santa Barbara Island which sits all by itself forty miles off the coast with wildlife and peace undisturbed. We were in familiar waters now, having sailed these islands for years on the El Viento before moving north to the job in Seattle.

These were the days when only an occasional fishing boat might stop at one of these outer island anchorages. More often than not, we were the only vessel there to share the abundance of sea life that thrived both on the islands and in the surrounding water. Great flocks of sea birds ranged overhead while huge herds of Sea Lions inhabited the rugged cliffs along the coasts. We could lie quietly on the edge of the rocks and look down into their rookeries without being detected. In the springtime the open mesa on Santa Barbara Island was the nesting ground for thousands of sea birds waiting for their eggs to hatch. If we ventured too close the ever attentive birds overhead would dive on us to show their displeasure at our unwanted intrusion.

For another week, we revisited familiar cruising grounds in the Channel Islands, then went on to our last stop at Catalina Island before heading for Newport Harbor, our temporary home for the next few months. There we would wait out our time and complete our obligations to the company. We knew there was much to do in making final preparations for the upcoming voyage, and we were full of anticipation. It just seemed too good to be true that we were in a position to get away from the workaday world and finally follow our dreams.

CHAPTER FIVE

AN OLD FRIEND WAITED IN Newport Harbor. Art Curtis offered us an empty slip in the Lido Peninsula Yacht Anchorage only a few hundred feet from where I first saw "Evening Star." We were happy to have such a beautiful place to spend the last few months of the year before our departure now scheduled for late December or early January. I had two major jobs to do on the boat. One was to install some kind of wind steering vane to relieve Jeanne and me of having to constantly be at the helm. The other was to devise some kind of a downwind rig for sailing dead before the wind which I anticipated most of our future sailing to be.

The first problem was easily solved. I contracted with a firm in Los Angeles to install an "Aries" vane made by a British company. It was thought to be the best in the world at that time, and I think that can still be said of it today. As it turned out, it did most of the steering on every point of wind for many thousands of miles. Every morning, when coming on deck for the first time, my crew would immediately inquire about the health of "Harry," a nickname they gave this wonderful device that saved them so much work. When they were satisfied he was OK, I might even rate a "good morning" myself.

For me, the other problem was not so easily solved. On the maiden voyage of "Evening Star" to Hawaii, I had only traditional fore-and-aft sails with no special rig for downwind sailing. It was a real pain trying to take a boat so rigged downwind in the trades. The problem, of course, is that you can fill only one sail when dead before the wind as that one sail is going to blanket the wind from hitting any other sail forward of it. Because of this the vessel is essentially crippled, limping along on one sail when you would like to have the power of three. The alternative is to follow a zig zag course, alternately sailing on one tack, then the other, far enough off the wind so as to broad reach with all sails full. This is not a satisfactory solution because of the much greater distance that has to be covered to get to your desired destination.

The so called "modern" way of solving the problem is by using a spinnaker, or twin headsails. Both have serious drawbacks. The spinnaker needs constant attention and a larger crew to set and keep it flying. The twin headsails are usually too small for a heavy vessel and require whisker poles to keep them full of wind. These poles can be a major headache and somewhat dangerous, in my experience, when jibed in heavy weather. Since a spinnaker rig was out of the question for me, I decided to install twin headsails as the only solution to my problem. I reached the decision reluctantly and without much enthusiasm. Then, one evening, I picked up a book by W. A. Robinson entitled, *To the Great Southern Sea*, and I knew I had another alternative, and the answer. A full page picture of his beautiful Brigantine, "Varua," under full sail off Tahiti gave it to me.

Why is such an obvious answer sometimes so elusive? The problem was solved hundreds of years ago in the early days of sail by using a square sail. It was the answer then, and in my opinion, it is still the best way to take a boat downwind if the vessel is heavy enough to handle the extra weight in the rigging. Robinson's "Varua" was a staysail schooner rigged square on the foremast, thus a Brigantine. To me, it's the ideal ship for offshore sailing because it is essentially two separate rigs. One can go before the wind under square sail and on the wind with the conventional fore and aft rig. I was excited, but how to adapt the square rig to my little ketch posed some problems. First, I wanted something that could be handled from the deck so as not to have to go aloft when setting it. The second was how to be able to brace the yard around when sailing somewhat off of dead downwind on a broad reach. I tackled the problem in total ignorance as it was just not done in these days and especially on a ketch rig.

First, I designed a bracing mechanism to hold the yard to the mast and pivot it both vertically and horizontally. I found a metal worker to help me in the design and to make the device out of stainless steel. Then, by the seat of my pants and common sense, I designed a yard arm that was twice the beam of the boat which became twenty-eight feet in length and tapered for the last seven feet at either end. A firm in Almitos turned the spar for me out of spruce and shipped it to our berth in the yacht anchorage.

That's when the problem began of having to listen to the laughs and jibes from the wharf sailors who thought I was crazy for doing such a thing to a beautiful ketch like "Evening Star." There were times when I had my own doubts, but I continued to try to make it work. It was a proud day when I finally hauled the yard up the mainmast and made it fast. From that day to this "Evening Star" took on a new personality and became the unique little vessel she is today. A large squaresail was ordered out of Hong Kong where they still knew how to make such monstrosities, and I also ordered a triangular Raffee to fly above it. There are skeptics still among my sailing friends, but none among those who have had the great experience of sailing with me on a downwind run with this beautiful rig, full and drawing.

CHAPTER SIX

By early December countdown to departure had begun. I didn't believe it could be so difficult to make the break from home, family, business ties, friends and the everyday world we had been a part of all our lives. Much later in our sailing life we could get up in the morning and decide on the spur of the moment to leave our present anchorage and be on our way by noon for a destination possibly a thousand miles away. For now though, an entry in my journal for December 8th is revealing:

"Early to bed this evening but a long time trying to get to sleep. Still doing a lot of soul searching, I guess. Also trying to plot a course for the next couple of years. Awfully hard to do. I hope my mind will clear somewhat once we are underway."

I worried about finances. We certainly were not in a position to retire and be financially secure for a long period of time. The company helped somewhat with a generous year-end bonus to ease the immediate cash flow problem. Past that, I had some vague idea that I was going to support us by writing or filming or. . . . Another immediate worry was my kids. Although I had been divorced from their mother for quite some time, we were close, and I knew they depended on me in many ways not the least of which was just to be available when needed. My oldest daughter, Chris, was in college and my son, Steve, was in the Navy, but Susie was still in Junior High School. Another excerpt from my journal just before departure:

"Chris came for dinner tonight on the boat and, again, we went over the financial arrangements for her college and personal needs. Then we said our final good-byes which wasn't easy, although I believe she and Susie have a healthy attitude about my being gone for awhile. I love them both so very much and I can't help but have a tinge of worry about their welfare while I am completely out of touch"

To go through a divorce where young children are involved is something you never really get over and you have to face the guilt when it hits you, which is often. I was particularly worried about Susie and made a strong bid to her mother to take her with us. It was no go, and I understood.

I had one solid rock to depend on. "Donis Leach" was my secretary of the past few years with the company. Actually, she was much more: a trusted friend, capable assistant and confidant, indispensable in helping me with my business activities. She was living in Seattle with her husband and new baby girl when we left for the South Pacific, and agreed to handle my correspondence and personal affairs and finances while I was away. I kept her informed of our schedule and itinerary, and she was the main link between us and our family and friends, receiving correspondence and forwarding mail. If one of my kids needed help or financial assistance, they called her. I owe a great debt of gratitude for her help and understanding of our situation during those years.

Jeanne's family was another concern. Her mother suffered from emphysema and was reluctant for us to leave on a long journey. They were very close and "Melba" came out to visit us for a few days in Newport Beach. She was a fine woman, full of spirit, who tried hard not to let her illness interfere with an active life. She was fun and we both loved her very much. She and Jeanne had a nice visit and I know the parting was difficult for both of them. Melba could have many years ahead of her with this debilitating illness but you just never know and when she left for home, she bravely wished us "Bon Voyage."

It is apparent why very few people do what I set out to do. Aside from not being emotionally able to take the risk of leaving career and financial security, they are unable to leave home and hearth. I have never honestly been able to answer the question: "Did I do it because I am stronger than other men or just weaker?" I am always reminded of lines in Robert Service's great poem, "The Men That Don't Fit In."

"And each forgets, as he strips and runs
with a brilliant, fitful pace,
It's the steady, quiet, plodding ones
Who win in the lifelong race."

Aside from personal problems, there are many other things to be concerned with. You are leaving grocery stores, hardware stores and every other means of obtaining tangible supplies for an unlimited and uncertain amount of time. It takes some real planning and soul searching to determine your needs. I wanted to be self-sufficient for a long period of time so that I would not have to cut short any opportunity to explore out- of-the way places because of the necessity to resupply the ship. We found the answer.

There was a new business beginning to emerge in a few locations; that of selling freeze dried foods. After some research and planning we purchased what would be almost a years supply of everything imaginable including meats, butter, eggs, vegetables, fruits, and all the staples. That, along with a case or two of powdered milk, could sustain us when we were completely out of touch with the means to secure fresh food. As it turned out, we only used this food when we were completely out of something else, but it proved to be the key to keeping us self-sufficient, and the best supplied vessel in the Pacific.

Surprisingly enough, a lot of the freeze dried things were pretty good and I also had the benefit of a very creative and excellent cook.

On December 12th Grant, and his wife, Suzanne, came to Newport for a visit. I was excited about seeing them and they insisted on taking us to dinner at a fancy Newport Beach restaurant. When we walked in, the Matre "d" ushered us in to a private dining room and there, already assembled at a banquet table, were company friends from all over the country. I am not easily surprised, but this going-away party was totally unexpected, and I was astounded. There was a lot of good-natured camaraderie during the evening, and Jeanne and I had a great time and were very grateful for the tribute. They presented me with a beautiful Tamaya sextant that was to be my daily companion on the afterdeck for the next few years as I worked to determine our position.

We were all nursing hangovers the next day, but after everyone caught planes for home, Grant and I had our final session for a long time. As a parting gesture he took me over to the shipyard and bought "Evening Star" a new "Dyer" sailing dinghy. We immediately commissioned it "USS Grant" and it would take us over many a reef and lagoon in the coming years. This dinghy still sits upturned on the foredeck and is a reminder that good friends of the calibre of this man are a rare gift in this day and age.

Medical supplies are a necessity on a voyage like this, and I was uncertain as to what I needed. On my bookshelf was a good book on the subject, written by Doctor "Peter Eastman." In looking over his book I noticed he lived in the Newport area, so I called him. What great good fortune. He and his wife came down to the docks to meet us and see the boat, and graciously put together a superb medical kit for us. I was very grateful, and it was plain that he and his wife were thinking about making a voyage of their own one day. His young son and new wife had already done so and the experiences and some medical problems they had encountered prompted the doctor to write his book for small boat sailors. There are a number of good first-aid books on the market but they tell you what to do until the doctor arrives. Doctor Eastman's book tells you what to do when there isn't a doctor on the horizon and you are on your own.

After a final haulout to paint the bottom, Christmas and New Year's were spent with family and friends and Jeanne and I had a last week with Susie at Catalina Island. There was nothing left to do but break the bonds of shore and start the odyssey we had been planning and dreaming of for so many years. Webster defines "odyssey" as "a long wandering marked usually by many changes of fortune." It was to be so for us.

PART TWO

In the South Seas

CHAPTER SEVEN

W E WERE READY TO GO but gale warnings had been up for two days with much heavy rain. Jeanne and I had spent a lot of time in our bunks reading and thinking about the warm southern ocean we would soon be heading into. Then, on the morning of January 8th, it was still raining but the winds were down to small craft warnings. We decided to leave.

As we powered down Newport Harbor in light rain, we realized we were the only vessel underway in this crowded marina of hundreds of boats. Big breakers and heavy seas pounded the breakwater and a strong southeast wind was still blowing. After rounding the harbor entrance buoy, we raised sail on a southwesterly course and held it for about an hour. Taking too much of a heavy sea off our port beam, I altered course and ran downwind for the east end of Catalina Island. Within a few hours we were in calm waters on the back side of the Island and headed for Cat Harbor to anchor for the night. The storm was dying and I looked for fair weather by morning. At least we were on our way.

The morning of January 9th dawned clear and beautiful as it always does after a storm, and when breakfast was finished we powered out of the harbor and headed southwest with the outline of San Clemente Island off our bow. Within an hour we left the calm waters close to the Catalina shore, picked up a bit of wind, and raised all sail. It was an exciting moment for us, and it turned out to be an interesting day. A Navy warship was firing at targets off the outer side of San Clemente island. Jet planes were taking off and landing. A helicopter flew over to check us out, and we passed large whales close aboard off the west end of the island. About sundown, the warship couldn't contain it's curiosity, I guess, and altered course heading our way. We had a brisk breeze by this time and all sails full. We must have made a beautiful picture driving through that blue sea with spume flying off our bow. I'm sure their Skipper knew from our course and distance offshore that we were headed for the South Pacific. They passed close off our beam and after a lot of waving from both crews, they altered course again and headed back. We continued on toward a sunset on the horizon.

Our ship's company contained more than just Jeanne and me. We had two cats named Salty and Shanghai that had been with us since they were small kittens. They were part of the family and gave us much pleasure as well as entertained us with their constant antics. They were fearless aboard the boat, it being the only home they had ever known. Every time we headed into the open sea after being in a harbor too long they suffered a brief bout of seasickness. When it was over, they were all over the vessel on one precarious perch or another. We tried not to worry about them when we were at sea but sometimes when one of them would disappear for a period of time a frantic search would ensue, both of us fearing the worst. Then, the little devil would turn up and I would want to kick him overboard. There are many places for a critter to hide on a little ship like ours. We've never lost a cat at sea although there have been a few aboard over the years. Cats make great boat pets, and they have certainly enriched our sometimes lonely existence.

The first week after leaving California was rather difficult. It was still the dead of winter in the northern latitudes and wind conditions changed frequently. This created a lot of work changing sails day and night but our course was mostly southerly and we ran down the latitude into warmer weather within a few days. On January 16th we were about the same latitude as the lower end of Baha, Mexico and becalmed on a warm quiet sea. I launched the rubber dingy and drifted around the boat just for some diversion. The cats piled in too. Within a short time there were a half dozen sharks swimming around the boat and we were entertained for awhile just watching them in the clear water. The cats were, of course, fascinated watching those large creatures so close. They loved fish and always wanted their share when we brought one aboard, but this was something else. When the dinghy was back aboard we turned on the engine to get us on our way again and charge batteries. The following day a slight breeze was in the making; just a few catspaws at first but then, within a few hours, we were at the edge of the northeast tradewinds.

For the next fifteen days the boat plowed a deep furrow in that bluest of Pacific waters with very little assistance from us. Harry, the windvane, did the steering. I was able to hang a lantern high in the rigging at night, go to bed for brief periods of sleep and wake up in the morning with a bow wave roaring and the boat steadily making it's way on our course. Because of concern and force of habit, I was up every couple of hours to check on things. It didn't hurt the night's rest though because I would be immediately asleep again when I returned to my bunk. We were out of the main shipping lanes in a remote part of the ocean. The days rolled by and our activities were pretty much the same on each one. Jeanne and I would clean the boat first thing before breakfast. A few buckets of sea water for the decks and a sweep down below. The cats were on deck immediately after first light to search for flying fish that had flown

31

into the sails at night and landed in the scuppers. They usually made a haul of several and had them half eaten in the cockpit well by the time I washed down. After breakfast I usually started the navigational chores by "shooting" the sun for a morning line of position. After plotting it, we would enjoy the morning on deck with a second cup of coffee and maybe do a little fishing. For people like us who enjoy sailing, the sea was forever entertaining. There were always the great sea birds and an occasional whale or large sea turtle to watch.

At high noon I would "shoot" the sun again as it reached it's meridian passage for a latitude shot, and by advancing my earlier line of position for the course and distance run between shots, I could cross the two and pinpoint our noon position each day. It was a high point of the day when I established it on the chart and we could see what our progress had been the past twenty-four hours. We would average about a hundred-and-twenty-five nautical miles a day; it was exciting to see the line drawn between noon positions crawl steadily toward our objective which was the Marquesas Islands, lying about eight hundred miles northeast of Tahiti.

By afternoon we were ready to get out of the sun and climb into a bunk to read. It was the first time in many years I could read for hours with nothing else on my mind but total absorption in a good book. The country we left behind was dealing with a stock market at an all time low, a fuel crisis worsening, the food industry threatening to go on strike and the government racked with indecision, chaos and the watergate scandal. We never looked back for fear all of that would overtake us.

The high point of the day at sea on any ship is the evening meal, and Jeanne always outdid herself in that department. We would both have a good refreshing bath after a day in the sun and then a pleasant cocktail hour. Tough life. I usually tuned into the Voice of America shortwave broadcasts to get the news while she fixed dinner. After that, with the lantern lit and hung high in the rigging, we turned in until morning, time to start another day. About every other day we would throw the heavy handline over the stern for fish and catch an occasional tuna or mahi mahi. When we were near the equator where the great yellowfin tuna run, I lost a line on two occasions and gave it up. We saw flying fish by the hundreds, but I don't care for them as a delicacy. For the cats, it was a different story and they stayed fat and happy.

On the evening of our 26th day at sea a celestial observation of the moon and the planet Venus put our position only about seventy-five miles from the island of Nuku Hiva. We were both getting excited about the coming landfall. The next morning at first light I awakened Jeanne to come on deck and view the bold outline of an island about fifteen miles away, broad on our port bow. It was "Ua Huka," and a few hours later "Nuku Hiva" hove into view. We rounded the southeastern tip of the island and looked at what is surely one of the most beautiful sights in the world. The mountains were a vivid green that dropped from sheer heights right into the sea, the greenery extending all the way to the water's edge. Spectacular is the only way to describe it. The first area we coasted was the Typee valley where Herman Melville experienced living among fierce cannibals for several months before escaping to Tahiti. His book *Typee* is an exciting tale. A few miles farther on the beautiful natural harbor of Taiohae Bay faced south toward a tradewind-whipped sea and with French and Quarantine flags flying, we entered and dropped anchor a hundred yards off the beach and village. The midday heat settled down upon us and I spread our awnings over the aft deck to give us some relief from the sun. We had arrived at our first south-sea island port. It was February 5th, my forty-fifth birthday.

CHAPTER EIGHT

THE MARQUESAS ISLANDS, far off the beaten track at the
eastern end of the Polynesian triangle, lie isolated and
beautiful just beyond the reach of the ever-expanding tourist
industry. A very complex, highly-developed society of Polynesian people had reached the pinnacle of their culture when
pacific explorers discovered these islands for the first time in
1591. It was a brief encounter, and it wasn't until almost two
hundred years later that explorers, whalers and later, missionaries in great numbers began to stop regularly at Nuku Hiva
because of the geographical proximity to the lush whaling
grounds of the Eastern Pacific and the fine natural harbor the
island provides. The result was nothing less than catastrophic
for the islanders. In 1774, when Captain Cook visited these
islands, it was estimated that over one-hundred-thousand
people lived there. By 1920, only some fifteen hundred survived the ravages of disease, pestilence, misguided religious
zeal and French occupation. In a sense, the islanders never
recovered. At the time of our visit in 1974, the population was
estimated to be about five thousand. A little later, Jeanne and
I wandered about the Typee Valley and observed the remnants
of a people that numbered over ten thousand in this valley

alone. Abandoned villages {where the only thing left is the great stone paepae which served as foundations for homes, temples and communal gathering places} were everywhere in the most lush surroundings imaginable.

At the moment, we were just happy to be in this out-of-the-way place, and we settled down in the shade of our aft deck to wait for someone to notice our quarantine flag and acknowledge our presence. In this great natural harbor there were only two other small sailing vessels, both flying the French flag. In a short time a bearded young Frenchman from the "St. George," one of the yachts, rowed over with a gift of fresh limes and greeted us. Fortunately, he could speak a little English and told us the local gendarme was very lax about the formalities and that we could go ashore at our leisure to clear with him. "Jean Louis" offered to go in with me the next morning to act as interpreter, and I readily accepted his offer.

The next day we stepped ashore for the first time in almost a month and presented ourselves to the French gendarme who was the sole authority on this large island. He was pleasant and efficient and with the help of "Jean Louis," we were given a three-months visa for French Polynesia. With the formalities out of the way, we walked the dirt road into the village that hugged the shore at the head of the bay. Behind the village the greenery climbed steeply into the lush mountains. The people we met along the way were friendly but somewhat shy and it wasn't easy to be too familiar with them quickly. As we proceeded down the single road that ran the length of the village, we came to the trading store belonging to Maurice McKittrick. He is the son of an English father and a Marquesan woman. Bob Mckittrick, his father, was a well known figure in these islands for many years until his death in 1968. He was a tattooed sailor from the old school and had served on board square-riggers in the days of sail, thrashing around the horn from England to Chili. I had read of this man in years past from the accounts of small boat sailors that had preceded us. He had

35

come to these islands almost fifty years before as a young man and had known them all from Gerbault to Harry Pidgeon to later arrivals like the Hiscocks. They all had one thing in common to say about him: He was a great spinner of yarns and I was sorry we were a few years too late to make his acquaintance.

Maurice greeted us warmly and inquired if we were off the ketch "Evening Star" riding at anchor in the bay and now plainly visible from his store. When I said we were, He produced two cold beers from his refrigerator and presented them to us. He said the trading schooner that stopped a few days before had brought him a letter from a young man by the name of Eastman. This was the young son, whom we had never met, of Doctor Eastman. He had sailed through here a few years before and met Maurice and was now writing to ask Maurice to welcome us with a brew when we arrived. His letter contained a couple of dollars. What a nice gesture and unexpected surprise!

Maurice remained a friendly and helpful man throughout our stay in Nuku Hiva supplying us with fresh fruit when we needed it. An evening he spent aboard the boat was very enjoyable, and we learned a lot about the islands from him. On the day we were to leave Taiohae Bay for other anchorages I stopped by his store and he pulled a book off his shelf to show me. This was *The Hidden Worlds of Polynesia* by Robert C. Suggs. He was an archaeologist who had spent months on Nuku Hiva in 1957 digging through the ruins of ancient villages to reconstruct their history and shed insight into their culture. I realized immediately this book was a treasure as I handed it back and expressed my disappointment at not borrowing it to read while I was there. Maurice shoved it back into my hands again and said, "Take it with you." I said, "But this is a book you should keep, Maurice. It is a history of your people." He said that would not be a problem. "I'll give you the name of a friend of mine who runs a Chinese store next to Quinn's Bar in Tahiti.

Just give it to him when you arrive and he will see that it is returned on one of the supply schooners." I was both thankful and overwhelmed at his generosity and trust. The book was a treasure and I read it eagerly as we travelled through the other islands. When I arrived in Tahiti a month later, I took the book to the Chinaman and left it with him. A year later I was back in Nuku Hiva, and there on the shelf in Maurice's store was the book. I guess there is still honor and trust in some parts of the world.

We enjoyed Taiohae Bay. A few other yachts stopped in from different parts of the world while we were there, and in these remote places you make friends easily. The island people are used to having yachts visit from time to time and they tend to ignore them and go about their routine. We found these people pleasant and friendly, but shy. Language, of course, was the insurmountable barrier and our inability to communicate was frustrating and disheartening. Jeanne and I tried to learn a little French before arriving but discovered that only the youngsters could speak it, so we concentrated on learning some words in Marquesan. A friendly greeting in their own language usually brought a smile and a much more favorable response than "Bonjour, Madame."

The colonialistic atmosphere prevailed and the French segregated themselves from the islanders almost completely. There was, consequently, no great affection between the two peoples. Other than the clearing formalities, we had nothing further to do with the French on the island ourselves. It wasn't by design; they just seemed also to ignore our presence. My limited exposure to the French people left me with the impression that they were somewhat vain and colorless. As for their efficiency in running the island government, they were exceptional.

A fine woman and true friend to all visiting sailors was "Hina." She was a huge woman with a great smile and gregarious manner, and she, her husband and oldest daughter joined us for a bash on the beach one night. The music and dancing they helped to provide was well worth the price of admission— one hundred francs—that we each chipped in to buy beef and bread for hamburgers. The beef was from wild cows that the islanders hunted in the interior of the island once a week, and the bread was from "Ropa," the half-pint Chinese-Tahitian baker who turned out some fairly respectable hamburger buns from his oven for the party. He was a true Island character, and each day he baked enough loaves of delicious French Bread to satisfy the needs of the village. In the afternoon, when the baking was done, he celebrated the event with beer or harder stuff. If you walked into his shed to buy bread you might easily find yourself with a glass of whisky and spend the whole afternoon unsuccessfully trying to pay for the bread. Occasionally he celebrated too much and the village substituted breadfruit for bread the next day.

After ten days the urge for quieter surroundings got the best of us and I hauled anchor and headed for the Typee valley only a few miles away. There we found ourselves alone in another beautiful natural harbor surrounded on three sides by spectacular greenery. At the head of the bay was a white-sand beach stretching from a line of coconut palms to the water with a fresh water stream running into the bay at one end. We could take our small boat up that stream and land ourselves just below the village to visit with the local inhabitants. There were only a few living in the valley, and the whole place had a mysterious air about it. I guess that was because we knew that a large teeming population of Polynesians lived on this very spot a couple of hundred years ago. We climbed on large stone paipai, the great foundations for homes and temples of the past, now all but buried in the heavy lush growth. There was also a tremendous amount of fruit growing that had once fed thousands. From our anchorage we could look back up the length of the valley that climbed into the mountains and see a large waterfall cascading from the heights. A glass of rum and dinner in the aft cockpit in

Sell your books at
sellbackyourBook.com!
Go to sellbackyourBook.com
and get an instant price quote.
We even pay the shipping - see
what your old books are worth
today!

the cool of the evening with that vista of beauty before us will long be remembered.

After a brief call again at Taiohae Bay to clear with the Gendarme, we sailed for the island of "Ua Po," about thirty miles away. This is a very small volcanic island and even more spectacular than Nuku Hiva with spires of limestone rock rising straight up hundreds of feet into the clouds. There are no natural harbors around the island, but we found a sheltered spot under a towering cliff that provided good protection on the western side. We anchored in eight fathoms in total solitude with not a sign of habitation anywhere. Jeanne and I immediately put on masks and fins and dove at the base of the cliff in the clearest of waters with tropical fish by the hundreds of every kind and color. But our solitude only lasted a day before outriggers appeared with a man and wife, sixteen year old boy and a baby. They came aboard at our invitation and Jeanne served them a lime punch and sweetbreads. The boy's name was Tex and he could speak a little English. With our growing number of words in his language, we were able to communicate a little. They insisted we come to their village and home for Kai Kai {eat} the following day, and we accepted. Tex came to the boat the following morning to take us to his home.

He showed up on the beach at the head of the bay and we rowed in. A horse was tied to a tree, and had been brought for Jeanne to ride. It seemed his village was in another valley and there was a high mountain- trail climb to get to it. The trail was so steep that Jeanne slid off the back of the horse as we started our climb. I was sweating and puffing when we reached the top and could see his village far below overlooking the sea. The panorama was breathtaking as we descended the winding trail to his home. The whole family, and there were many children, was involved in preparing the meal of breadfruit and fish in many different ways. Jeanne and I had brought fresh bread from Rapa's oven and a jug of wine. When all was ready, they invited us to sit down and eat while they just sat around the perimeter of the table and watched. It's strange, but that's the way islanders treat guests. We were their entertainment. They knew the foods were strange to us and they watched with intense interest to see how we reacted. I was always courting disaster at one of these feeds as the food was not for my palate and the flies were a problem, but Jeanne saved the day as she tried everything and raved about them with great good spirit. The kids suffer from open wounds of coral poisoning and I knew where those flies had been prior to landing on the food. During our stay at the island we met many of the people, ferried them back and forth between villages for various reasons, and visited them in their homes. Their music is delightful, played on guitars and home made ukuleles. One of the "ukes" was presented to me as a gift by a village school teacher and was a treasured memento of our stay in this friendly place. After two weeks, we departed the island on a beautiful sparkling morning heading southwest. As those incredible spires disappeared below the horizon I wondered if we might ever pass this way again.

CHAPTER NINE

TAHITI LAY EIGHT-HUNDRED MILES AWAY, and directly in our
path to the fabled isle were the low atolls of the Tuamoto
Archipelago. It is always dangerous to navigate through these
islands because of strong unpredictable currents and the difficulty in seeing an atoll from the deck of a small ship until you
are practically on the reefs surrounding them. The easy way
would have been to skirt the islands to the north but I wanted
to visit at least one of the atolls if possible, so we held our
southwesterly course for several days. Late in the afternoon of
our fourth day at sea, I placed our position ten miles northwest
of the little island of Manahi. Later, I came topside from a nap,
and Jeanne was anxiously scanning the horizon for some sign of
the atoll. I climbed to the yardarm for a better look, and within
a few minutes the island was clearly visible and close aboard.

With the big squaresail drawing and a light tradewind dead
aft, we coasted the atoll and enjoyed the scenery in the last light
of day. I hove to on the starboard tack with reduced sail, and as
night came on we were slowly drifting with the current and
forereaching away from the reef. At daylight next morning, the
island was still there and only a few miles away. I raised all sail
and headed for the lee side of the island. There was a small pass

into the lagoon and next to the pass was the only village on the island with a population of about two hundred. I stood off the pass until near slack water and then headed in for the village. There was a gathering of people standing on a layer of concrete poured on top of the vertical face of the reef which served as a quay. They took our lines as we came alongside and for the first time since leaving California, we were actually tied up to the land. I was uneasy at first about being so close to a jagged reef but the constant tradewind kept us off it and we lay there next to the village for five days. Since we were the only boat to visit for several months, they welcomed our intrusion.

I stepped ashore and there was a small open boat a few yards ahead of us that was preparing to take some of the villagers to another motu on the reef to work copra. A young man was sitting on the stern working on their outboard motor. I watched for a few minutes and could see he was filing a rusty nail that was much too small and too weak to use as a shearpin. It had already broken once as they tried to leave. I took him aboard my vessel and we found some strong rod that was the right size. In half an hour, I made him a good shearpin and a couple of spares. It was a good way to begin our visit.

Later in the afternoon, Jeanne and I took a walk to stretch our legs. The whole island was only half a mile long and a couple of hundred yards wide. At the other end of the motu there was a break in the reef and we met a man with his wife and kids fishing. He turned out to be "Huri," the chief of the island and our most gracious host and constant companion for the next few days. He was a fascinating man about thirty-five years old and very intelligent, with a desire to learn everything he could about the boat and navigation. His most prized possession was a small pickup truck the French government had left him. Why, I don't know. There were only a few hundred yards on the whole island on which to drive. It had not run in quite some time and I managed to help him fix it which made him, and especially the kids, very happy. They loved to ride around in the back of the thing.

There was a constant procession of people aboard the boat and we entertained them as best we could, knowing there was not a lot of diversion to break the monotony of their lives. In gratitude, Huri brought an older man aboard one day to present me with a gift. It was a solemn occasion and we sat below in the main salon. He produced a large shell with a pearl still attached in the middle of it and I was highly pleased and honored. We made a frame and it still hangs today on the bulkhead of the main cabin. Later, I asked Huri what would be an appropriate gift for the man in return. He said, "Do you have any aspirin? He is a retired diver who hurt his ears on deep dives and suffers frequently from headaches." The gift of a large bottle of aspirin and a bone fishing jig was a welcome present for the old man. These people in the out islands did not have any medicines and could only rely on a short wave radio to notify the French authorities of any problems. We shared things from our medical chest on many occasions.

On the afternoon of our fifth day on Manahi, the wind shifted and an angry swell began to build on the reef just outside our anchorage. We hastily said our good-byes and the islanders cast off our lines. The current carried us quickly out of the pass and we set sail, again heading southwest. With a good breeze to drive us, the little island disappeared as quickly and dramatically as it had appeared out of the ocean a week before.

The following morning, I had another of the Tuamoto Islands ahead of us but the British Pilot book warned against trying to land on it. Rangiroa, the largest Island of the group, lay fifty-five miles away and I toyed with the idea of heading there, but the prospect of arriving at night and the black squalls then building all around us changed my mind. We bore away for Tahiti, now only a few days sail away. The tradewind fell light and it was near midnight of the third day when I sighted Venus

Light through intermittent rain showers and about fifteen miles distant. The following morning, we viewed the great green island of Tahiti sparkling in the early rays of the sun. We slipped through the pass in the reef at Papeete and entered this most famous of all south sea island ports. Sailing vessels from all over the world were tied up Tahiti style, bow anchor out and stern lines tied to large bolyards set firmly in the grass along the waterfront. The colorful town stretched out along the shore with verdant green mountains for a backdrop. By the time we set our bow anchor and backed in close to the shore, a group of Tahitians and other boat crews were gathered to help. I heaved a stern line toward them and we were soon ashore ourselves, laughing and swapping stories with other sailors. To sail to this fabled place in my own vessel was the culmination of a long-held dream and I relished it.

CHAPTER TEN

AFTER SEVERAL MONTHS in the remote islands, Tahiti was somewhat of a letdown for us. The fabled isle was not exactly what we expected it to be, thanks to the invention of the jet airplane. The dusty waterfront of days gone by with schooners backed up to the quay and laughing curious island-ers mingling with the sailorfolk was a thing of the past. Instead, there were the usual great number of tourists, hundreds of cars and motor scooters and the resulting gas fumes drifting across the boats anchored at street level. It was still Tahiti though, an Island of incredible beauty. The central marketplace in down-town Papeete on an early morning was still old Tahiti with every kind of locally produced food and fresh fish right from the sea. The colorful dress of the throngs of Islanders and the mingling smells of flowers and fish was a tapestry of Island culture. We spent the first week sight-seeing and writing letters but soon tired of the crowds and longed for quieter anchorages. After haunting the post office for another week waiting for mail that never came, we decided to leave for the leeward islands of the Society group.

With the wind vane set and steering, Jeanne and I worked hard for several hours scrubbing the muck of Papeete harbor off our mooring lines and chain. We passed by the beautiful island of Moorea, renowned for it's lush tropical beauty, but feared it would be too much like Tahiti and sailed on. That night remains in my memory as one of the most delightful I have ever experienced at sea. With a moderate tradewind blowing off our quarter and a big moon to light the way, we sailed westward toward the Island of Huahine. I couldn't bring myself to give up the deck watch so I stayed up most of the night before reluctantly calling Jeanne to relieve me. To be able to sit on deck late at night in the Southern Tropics, perfectly comfortable in a pair of thin shorts and barefooted, is an experience we seldom have in the Northern Hemisphere. Add to that the pleasure of viewing new constellations that never appear above the horizon in our country and you have some idea of the fascination those tropical nights held for us. Later, as we moved northward again, we were to miss the sight of the Southern Cross as it rose out of the sky each night followed by Scorpio with it's brilliant red eye, "Antares." This is sailing at it's very best and it was with some disappointment that Jeanne awakened me shortly after daybreak and announced that the island of Huahine was in sight and not very far distant.

By mid morning, we skirted the palm covered northern end of the island and entered a quiet harbor on the leeward side through a wide break in the fringing reef. Our anchor went down in five fathoms of clear water and could easily be seen digging into the white sand on the bottom. This was another high island with green mountains and still lagoons and was quite beautiful. After getting the boat in shape and our sun awnings up, we launched the dinghy and rowed a few hundred feet to the beach. Palms grew almost to the water's edge and there were graves of some long dead missionaries along the path that led a quarter of a mile to the little town of "Fare." We followed the path to find the local gendarme to present our papers and passports. As it was siesta time, he came to the door of his house sleepy-eyed and suggested we leave our papers and return tomorrow.

Huahine was one of my favorite islands. It was small, off the beaten track with hardly any tourists, and it had a beautiful anchorage and great diving on reefs close by. There was a new, small hotel near our anchorage preparing for the coming tourist trade but with almost no guests at the time. For entertainment, a few of the local musicians gathered there in the evenings to play and sing just for the fun of it. It was all so informal and enjoyable. The little town of Fare was exactly what most of us envision a South Sea's town to be. It sat in a corner of the quiet peaceful lagoon with one main road along the tree-lined waterfront. Island trading vessels docked on the concrete quay across the road from the stores and unloaded their cargo. The sight of piles of large melons, which Huahine was famous for, along with stacks of sacked copra, added to the colorful panorama of the waterfront. The rich aroma of copra, tropical flowers and sweating people, is the South Pacific. There was one freshwater spigot on the quay and we took our turn washing clothes and filling water jugs with the dinghy tied a few feet away. Just to be a part of the activity and informality of it all captivated us. This is what we had travelled such a long road to see and experience.

A few days later, Jeanne and I were enjoying our nightly cocktail on deck when a friend we had met earlier waved from the beach with what looked like a letter in his hand. I rowed in and he gave me a four day old telegram from Jeanne's father telling us of her mother's death. It was a great shock and a saddening experience for both of us, especially hard for Jeanne, being so far away and not knowing any of the details. She was very close to her mother and her passing left a deep void of love and companionship that would be forever missed. In the quiet beauty of a tropical evening, we toasted the memory of this fine lady and wept.

Four days later, we sailed for Bora Bora less than fifty miles away and arrived late in the afternoon. Jeanne managed to get to the post office in the main village before it closed and picked up the mail that had eluded us in Papeete a month before. Two letters from "Shirl," Susie's mom, brought distressing news. There was a note of panic in them as she described some of the problems our daughter was having since entering Junior High School. My help was obviously needed so a change of plans began to take place. We were only two-thousand miles away from New Zealand, with the Cook Islands, Tonga, Samoa and Fiji in between. These islands had been our likely destinations up to this point. The upwind trip to Hawaii was not a pleasant alternative, but under the circumstances, it was the way we chose to go. The western Pacific Islands would have to wait.

Bora Bora was an absolute paradise and for the next ten days we stayed there and enjoyed the good life. They were lazy days of diving, shelling, reading and writing letters. We were anchored off a large motu inside the great fringing reef surrounding the island in total solitude amid dazzling beauty. Before leaving for Hawaii, we moved over to the island of Raiatea for a few days to get provisions and see what it was like.

On a brilliant morning, we sailed most of the length of the great lagoon that encircles the islands of Raiatea and Taha. By early afternoon, we were through the pass on the northwest end of the island and heading north. The islands of Raiatea, Taha and Bora Bora were prominent astern all the rest of the day, but at first light the following morning, they had dropped out of sight below the horizon. We were close-hauled on the wind for the first time in many months and Honolulu lay almost twenty-five hundred miles away. After only two days of moderate winds, we sailed into a particularly wicked-looking squall and I changed to a smaller working jib and reefed the mainsail in anticipation of some heavy wind. We passed through the squall but the wind and seas remained for the next two-thousand miles to Hawaii. It was to be an uncomfortable twenty days of pounding into wind and seas before reaching our destination. Just before dawn of our twentieth day out of Raiatea, we lined up the range lights of Ala Wai Harbor in Honolulu and entered through the narrow channel. It was a welcome relief to anchor in a quiet spot behind the breakwater to await customs and agriculture inspectors to board.

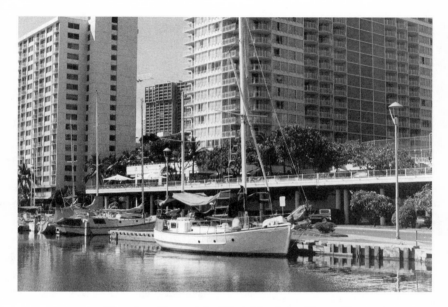

Evening Star, Ala Wai Harbor, Hawaii

CHAPTER ELEVEN

"EVENING STAR" LAY AT ANCHOR in Ala Wai Harbor for a month. The anchorage was near the rock jetty across from the fuel dock with all the activity of Waikiki Beach a short walk away. Jeanne flew home to be with her father for a couple of weeks and Susie came out from California to join the ship. It gave us some time alone to deal with her problems and it wasn't easy. These were troubled times for American youth and I found it hard to deal with the peer pressure. I could not accept the premise that a thirteen-year-old was now able to deal with life in a mature manner and make her own decisions. I had gone through this with my son and lost. He quit school before finishing high school and was now in the Navy but I worried about his future in a competitive world without a proper education. I was determined not to let this happen with Susie. I took a firm stand and there was a lot of resentment at first. It was an uncomfortable relationship for awhile but gradually improved as her renewed respect for me deepened and mine for her. We were always father and daughter but eventually became friends again as time progressed.

Our stay in Honolulu was made more pleasurable because of the presence of two families we had known on the mainland who now both lived on boats in the marina. Don and Diana Anderson had two daughters Susie's age which made it nice for her. Ken and Dawn Murray were good friends also whom we had met while Jeanne and I had the boat in Oxnard. All of us left Southern California about the same time for different parts of the world. Don and Diana sailed across the Pacific to Australia with their two small daughters and Ken and Dawn went down the coast to Mexico, Panama and eventually the Galapagos Islands. We had gone to Seattle to follow my business career, but now circumstances brought us back together in Honolulu. Ken Murray was one of my closest personal friends and was especially helpful to me. He took us everywhere in his old car to run errands and see the sights of the Island and we enjoyed his company.

One quiet morning, we hauled anchor and headed for an overnight sail to the Island of Kauai, ninety miles away. Rounding the northern tip of the Island in the early afternoon of the following day, we entered the pleasant harbor at Hanalei Bay and anchored off the beach where scenes from the movie "South Pacific" were shot some years ago. By now, a new plan had taken shape. I had wanted to see Alaska since I was a kid, but somehow never made it. Here it was, within easy reach of our sailing vessel at the peak of the summer season, so we decided to go for it. At this time, not many private yachts made this trip. The short summer season and the possibility of gales and heavy weather in the North Pacific was the reason. I planned our trip carefully to have us back in Seattle before Labor Day and in California before the real winter weather set in. Our final destination was still the South Pacific Islands and we expected to be headed there again by the end of the year.

Hanalei Bay is another of my favorite places. It is a huge bay with a wide sand beach almost a mile long stretched out in a crescent shape around the head of it. The large hotels hadn't found their way there yet and it was a quiet anchorage with not many people on the beach, and the little town of Hanalei a short walk away. A river ran into the bay at it's head and we could take a small boat up the river toward the inland mountains for several miles. Towering cliffs behind the town, with numerous waterfalls cascading into the valley below, completed the picture.

Our stay was brief because of the urgency in reaching Alaska at the peak of the summer season, but I made a new friend. A broken fan belt on the engine needed a replacement and I was on the road that led out of Hanalei to the main town of Lihue at the other end of the Island. An older gentleman picked me up and we struck up a conversation. He was a retired Navy Captain and we discovered that his best friend, also a Navy Captain, was my former commanding officer when I was in the Navy stationed at Hickam Field. I was somewhat of a maverick in those days and had found myself in a bit of trouble. My C. O. had been lenient with me when I went before him at "Captain's Mast," which was just a hearing to determine if the problem was serious enough to warrant a court martial. In my case, the Captain resolved the matter by transferring me to the Island of Guam, some thirty-five-hundred miles away. In doing so, he both punished and saved me at the same time. I had never forgotten it and when I related the story to this gentleman, he said that was typical of his old comrade who was somewhat of a maverick also and sometimes in hot water with his superiors. My new friend drove me to Lihue, helped me find the fanbelt and returned me to the boat. I invited him and his wife out to the boat for cocktails, and in the next few days, we visited them in their home on the beach and became better acquainted. When we were ready to leave for Alaska, he presented me with a large sack of hardwood, all cut up into nice sized pieces to fit the small fireplace on the boat.

We left Kauai heading north, and for ten days had beautiful sailing up through the Northeast Trades, through the Horse Latitudes and into the Westerlies. An excerpt from my journal of July 14th:

"Sunday, superb day. Clear sunshine in the morning and fog in the afternoon. Brisk following wind with the Squaresail and Raffee set. Jeanne and Susie baked all day. I fixed hatch doors, tore into the bilge pump and fixed it. Hauled in a nice Albacore this afternoon and had fish for dinner. Beginning to get cold in the evenings so we dug out our coats and built our first fire in the fireplace."

From here on, we experienced pure North Pacific weather of some sunshine but a lot of fog and overcast days. We read, played cards, ran the ship and plowed north toward Alaska. Early on the morning of our twentieth day out of Hawaii, we saw the tops of high mountains through patchy fog and overcast. Then, shortly after noon, we made our landfall at Cape Spencer and entered the wide mouth of Cross Sound, the northern-most entrance to the inside waters of southeast Alaska. The magnificence and beauty of that big country became immediately apparent as we suddenly viewed snow-covered mountains, deep fjords and the blue-white ice of our first glacier falling into Taylor Bay off to our port side. About

Susie at the helm

Heavy weather

three miles inside Cross Sound, we turned South and entered Lisianski Inlet, a deep fjord-like channel about a mile wide in most places. Under power, we followed this beautiful waterway for twelve miles with steep mountains and green virgin forests on either side of us. As the late afternoon sun disappeared over the ridge to starboard and long shadows fell over the waterway, we rounded a bend and slowly coasted toward the rough hewn log docks of the little town of Pelican, Alaska.

This town of about one-hundred-and-fifty people is built into the base of a wooded mountain that rises almost vertically from the water. In fact, the town is built entirely over the water with a long wooden pier on pilings serving as the main street. The houses stretch out along one end of the pier while the fish processing plant, cold storage and a few stores dominate the other end with the docks below. This was the height of the fishing season and there was much activity as boats were constantly coming in to unload their catch. Small float planes, the town's main link with the outside world, would occasionally land in the quiet waters and taxi up to the docks to unload passengers and freight. A sailing boat was a novelty here, especially one recently out of the South Pacific, and we had many visitors aboard. I was asked to present a slide show of our travels at the local town hall and I complied. I think everyone in town was there. They had recently started a new library and I donated a volume from my own shelves in gratitude for their hospitality. Alaska was still an uncluttered wilderness with great natural beauty and friendly people who had a tremendous pride in their domain. Their pioneer spirit and open friendliness was as refreshing as the country itself.

From Pelican, we made our way to the very northern end of Glacier Bay where several live glaciers could be viewed and huge chunks of ice, sometimes weighing tons, frequently fell into the bay a few hundred yards from the boat. As we slowly threaded our way through icebergs, we picked up small pieces from the water and filled our ice chest. The ice was so hard it had not absorbed salt water, and for two weeks, it was a distinct pleasure to pour my nightly rum ration over glacial ice at cocktail time. There was very little wind for sailing in these inland waters and our engine was used most of the time for running. The tides and currents in these latitudes are to be reckoned with and the tidal current books were our daily companions. The summer days were quite long and the sun never set before 9 P.M. so it gave us plenty of time for long runs during daylight hours. We never ran at night and frequently anchored in a quiet wooded spot at the head of one of the many streams flowing into the Sound. The fishing was excellent and we never casually threw a line in without expecting to do battle. Salmon were plentiful and with a small amount of special fishing gear and a little help from the locals on how to use it, we were able to take them trolling. At almost any anchorage, the Halibut would start biting as soon as a jig reached the bottom.

The Alaskan Brown Bear can be a real menace in this country and we were cautious in our brief exploring trips to the woods around our anchorages. We saw many signs of bear but had no actual encounters. To see a freshly made bed in the damp grass the size of a pickup truck was enough to start the adrenaline flowing and the hair on the back of my neck to stand up. The knowledgable people in these parts never go unarmed into the woods and sometimes wear heavy sidearms when wading and fishing the streams. The healthy respect these people show for this huge animal was enough to convince me the menace was real. One evening, in a remote anchorage at the head of a river, we had gone to bed when I heard an eerie cry in the night. Thinking it might be some wild animal, I carefully eased the hatch open and took a look outside. The cry came again and sounded like it was right next to the boat so I grabbed a flashlight and took a look. There in the water next to the boat was Shanghai, one of the cats, struggling to stay afloat. He had fallen overboard. I don't know how long he had been in the cold water but he was almost gone, and when he rolled over with his head out of the water, that awful sound emerged from him. I grabbed a net and scooped him from the water but he appeared limp and almost dead with his eyes rolled back. I told Jeanne and Susie to get a wood fire going in the fireplace quickly and we soon had the cat stretched out in front of it soaking up the heat. I stroked the water from his lungs and, to our surprise, he slowly began to revive. Within an hour, he was running around playing with "Salty" like nothing had happened. We were thankful and happy to have our little shipmate back in good health.

From Glacier Bay, we worked our way eastward to Juneau where the famous Mendenhall Glacier is fed by an enormous ice field just above the city. Our anchorage was actually in Auke Bay, a suburb northwest of the main part of town. We remained there for a week and I was engaged most of the time in repairing a faulty heat exchanger on the engine. Had I not been so preoccupied with this chore, we would have made the trip by ferry a hundred miles north to Skagway and from there, overland by narrow gage railway, to Whitehorse and the Yukon gold fields. We were told it was a beautiful trip and an excellent chance to glimpse some of the historical Alaskan past.

From Juneau, we moved south to Ketchikan, our last stop in the state. It is the gateway to Alaska and a busy fishing and shipping port. From there, we threaded our way eight-hundred miles south through the inside passage to Seattle for a brief visit with old friends. Then, out the Strait of Juan De Fuca and south for California, just ahead of the coming winter. On September 7th, we sailed under the Golden Gate Bridge to complete a near circumnavigation of the Eastern Pacific that had taken us from Tropical Islands to Glacial ice. Our goal was still the Southwest Pacific and we settled down to prepare for another run at it.

Susie and Jeanne

CHAPTER TWELVE

IT WAS A FEW DAYS AFTER CHRISTMAS when Jeanne, Susie and I left Southern California, again, headed for the Marquesas Islands. The kittens were not with us, having been given to another family on a large boat in San Francisco Bay. We missed them but some of the places we planned to visit didn't accept pets and we were afraid they would present too much of a problem. Our first landfall was at "Hiva Oa" in the southern group of the Marquesas Islands. We arrived just before evening twilight after a twenty-three day voyage from California and anchored in a little bay adjacent to the main village of "Atouna."

We spent almost two weeks there getting reacquainted with the tropics. As usual, the people were great and Susie received her first taste of life in the South Seas. The head of the bay was a luxuriant garden with high palms and heavy tropical growth so dense that we had to wade the river running through it to make headway on our excursions inland looking for fresh limes and bananas. This same valley was the battleground of cannibals less than one-hundred-and-fifty years ago when the people of Atouna and the neighboring village of "Haamau" were at continual war with each other. The eyewitness accounts of human killings and cannibal feasts, as related to Robert Louis Stevenson when he visited this bay aboard the schooner "Casco" in 1889, makes interesting reading. In those days, this valley was a no-man's land between the two waring factions, and today, it is still empty of human habitation. The village of Atouna is the place where the French painter, Paul Gauguin finally retreated to spend the last years of his life. One afternoon, we climbed up to the cemetery high on a hill behind the village to visit his grave site and view the beautiful panorama looking seaward from this lonely spot.

From "Hiva Oa," we sailed southwest to the most southerly of the Marquesas Isles, "Fatu Hiva." We found ourselves becalmed off the leeward side of the island at sunset with an engine that heated up after only a few minutes running, so we hove to for the night. Winds were light most of the following day also, and it was almost evening again before we worked our way to an anchorage. It was worth the trouble. As the sun went down, we just stared at an unbelievable Hollywood-like setting before us. High, wooded cliffs with a carpet of green dropped into the small bay on either side. A sand beach complete with a stream running into the bay was in front of us with a carpeted path of green grass leading up the slight incline toward the village. Behind the village, the valley narrowed with towering lava cliffs on either side, through which the small stream poured from the higher mountains inland. It was another spectacular south sea island setting and we never tired of looking at it.

For a few days, we visited with the villagers and walked the paths which followed the stream into the heart of the island. One night, a casual walk into the village turned into singing and dancing along the rock-lined walkway that formed the main road. We could have spent more time in this lovely place but after four days, we raised our anchor and sailed away. Most of the glowing accounts of south sea islands never mention the unpleasant aspects of these places but there was one here. A small black pesky species of fly nearly drove us nuts, even insulated as we were by being anchored offshore. So it was with both regret and relief that we left. With a fresh breeze to fill our sails, we headed for the island of Tahuata, forty miles away.

Again, the wind fell light as we approached the island and I worked into a very poor anchorage in the last light of day. There, we spent an uncomfortable night of rolling and anchor watching. The following morning, we got underway and worked our way in light air along the lee side of the island to the small village of "Hapitoni." The whole population of this little place was about twenty five and they gathered on a grassy knoll as we slowly worked our way to an anchorage a few yards in front of them. The water was crystal clear and we dropped our anchor in among the mushroom coral that dotted the bottom. One of our most pleasant weeks was spent here with the two families that the village comprised. A couple of young girls took charge of Susie almost immediately and we didn't see her for the rest of the week. The chief presented us with a stalk of bananas when I met him and soon our decks were stacked with young drinking coconuts that we continued to use all the way to the Tuamoto Islands.

Jeanne and Susie did a much needed washing at one of the houses where they had a source of running water, and I visited with the men. The chief's house at the end of the village had a generator which needed fixing so we tackled the job. After it was repaired, I set up my movie projector by the house and hung a white sheet up for a screen. For several nights, we watched the Disney movies I had brought along, their favorite being "Twenty Thousand Leagues Under The Sea." Another sailing yacht stopped by while we were there and, luckily, they had a part I needed to repair the saltwater pump on my engine. Just before leaving, Jeanne performed a not uncommon service for these people. Previous visiting boats had written letters to them which they couldn't read so she spent one morning translating and writing replies for them. We took these with us to mail at the next landfall with a post office.

We sailed back to the northern group of the Marquesas to show Susie the places we had visited before and to visit with Maurice McKittrick again at his store in Taiohae bay. After ten days in the northern islands, we followed our track of a year ago to "Manahi" in the Tuamoto islands before sailing on for Tahiti. It was late in March when we tied up again on the waterfront in Papeete only a few yards from our anchorage of the previous year. We only stayed a couple of weeks before picking up three-month-old mail from the post office and moving to the island of Moorea which we bypassed the year before. When we anchored in Robinson's Cove with our stern line tied to a coconut tree ashore and saw how pretty it was, we realized we had made a mistake not stopping here the first time. It was truly a beautiful place, only a few miles away from Tahiti. One of the letters we opened was unique because it was from the cats, Salty and Shanghai. It read:

Dear Mom and Dad,

So much has happened since Christmas that we really don't know where to start. I [Salty] can't say that we've been perfect boys but we sure have tried. We fought a couple of times and I fell in the water once and once we couldn't find Shanghai anywhere. He was hiding somewhere and only after a frantic search did he show up. He won't tell us where he was hiding because it's his secret. The skipper made us a pretty little house in an overturned box with a soft blanket inside. Shanghai is really wild over it and I guess it's nice but I like to sleep in one of the bunks instead. My favorite bunk is Mrs. Lacert's. She does not like it at all since I leave cat hairs all over the place so she picks me up and puts me in Marie Claude's bunk. The weather up here is really wet. We are also travelling a little. We are staying in Barkley Sound and anchored in a quiet place. Well, we have it pretty easy around here but we miss you very dearly. Home is home after all.

Your boys, Salty and Shanghai

What a nice gesture. The Lacerts were from the Puget Sound area and had a large vessel, "Marabel," about one-hundred-thirty-six feet long. When we met them in San Francisco, they agreed to take the cats as pets for their young daughter who wanted them badly. We knew they would be in good hands. It seemed silly to keep up correspondence with a couple of alley cats but Jeanne loved it.

After spending time in Moorea and the other leeward islands of the Society group, we were ready to move on to something new. On April 15th, we sailed through the pass at Bora Bora and headed west toward the Cook Islands. I wanted to stop at Suvarov atoll and visit with Tom Neal, a hermit who had lived on the island for some years. He had written a book called "An Island To Myself" and I had it in my library aboard. He was a New Zealander who had opted for the subsistence life on an isolated atoll and was now about seventy years old. We raised the island eight days out of Bora Bora and studied the pass into the lagoon. There was no chart and it was shallow with many coral heads along the fairway. With Jeanne at the helm, I climbed into the rigging and, standing on the yard, guided her through the pass and around to the lee of Anchorage island. It was just a small motu on the reef and we anchored in quiet water not far off shore.

We met Tom on the sand beach when we rowed in and he was cordial as he invited us to his house. The whole island was only a few hundred yards long and a hundred or so wide. His house was a little two room affair with a small covered porch, made out of driftwood and materials from boats that had been wrecked on the reef. A couple of small shacks nearby , one being his cooking shed, completed his living compound. He also had a small garden which he was very proud of. Tom was an interesting man; well-read and educated, but wore only a loin cloth at his island home. When we invited him to our boat for dinner, he came dressed like an English gentleman.

I asked him about a large open boat lying upturned on the beach and he said he had salvaged it off the reef but it was beyond repair as there was a huge hole in the chine. I told him I might have the necessary materials aboard to repair it if he wished to try. He gladly accepted my offer and we worked for a week repairing the hull. It was an icebreaker for me. After all, he was a hermit who liked his privacy and I would probably not have spent much time with him had it not been for our project. The boat was really not of any use to him because it weighed several hundred pounds and was too heavy for one man to handle, but he said he might trade it to a passing ship. We spent an enjoyable week at Suvarov and took the dingy to explore other small islands around the lagoon. The whole atoll was uninhabited and quite off the beaten track. I learned a few years later that a passing boat had found Tom dying and removed him from the island. He was one of those few men who lived and died doing his own thing rather than being a victim of circumstance. I made my own chart of the island before I left and have it in my chartroom still, just in case I ever go back.

American Samoa lay to the west and we shaped a course for there after leaving Suvarov. Five days later, we entered the big harbor of Pago Pago and tied up to the quarantine dock to go through the formalities. The officials were not friendly and close to rude as they cleared us into the port. This was a beautiful natural harbor hemmed in on three sides by mountains and greenery, but there was a feeling of tension in the place. Part of it was caused by a large population of Korean fishermen on one side of the harbor that the Samoans held animosity for, creating an uncomfortable atmosphere. We stayed only a week before moving on. One thing we did find, however, was American goods at cheap prices so we reprovisioned the ship and took on fuel. Less than a week later, we were again at sea headed for the kingdom of Tonga.

CHAPTER THIRTEEN

Tonga is the last surviving kingdom of the South Seas. They were never taken over by the colonial powers and remained a separate culture, unchanged by the western world. The islands are of raised coral and the people live simply in small villages on the different islands. They don't have much in the way of material goods but they have plenty to eat from the sea and green vegetables that they raise in communal gardens they call their "bush." The bush is a common area of each village, owned and maintained by all members of the community. A king still rules over a benevolent society.

After only a four-day sail from Samoa, we entered the northern group of islands and made our way through narrow channels to the little town of "Neafu." When you enter Tonga, you know you are in a different world from other South Pacific islands. There is a feeling of serenity, so unlike the westernized culture of Samoa we had just left. The officials were friendly and helpful and the people all smiles and gracious to each other, and to us. The anchorage was poor in front of the town so, after checking in and getting a good night's rest, we headed back to a small island that looked promising when we passed it the day before. There was good holding ground just off the island and we dropped anchor, spread our awnings and prepared to enjoy a few days in this peaceful place. We were next to a causeway that separated two small islands. On one, a village of maybe a dozen families lived on a grassy knoll and on the other was their bush that supplied food for the village.

The next morning, I was working on deck and could see a hollowed-out log with a single individual slowly making its way against the current toward the boat. The current was rather strong and the canoe was not making much headway but the individual sat unconcerned and stroked the water with a makeshift oar. Actually, it wasn't an oar at all, just a flat piece of board. I continued working and waited for him to approach. The middle-aged man was all smiles when he finally reached the boat and I dropped him a line and invited him aboard. He could speak very little English but his name was "John" and we became great friends. He was the only single man in the village and when I asked him why he never married, he said, "I like to take a walk." This literally meant, he wanted to be free to do his own thing. He was like an uncle to all the kids in the village and introduced Susie to some of the young girls her age. They were a happy people and Susie and a couple of the girls became great friends. They rode ponies around the island, took her to church on Sunday and had her spend the night in their homes. The homes were simple affairs with thatched roofs and dirt floors covered with beautiful hand woven mats. The few days we planned to spend in this spot turned into two weeks as we settled into the life of the village.

The movie projector was a great hit as usual. We would go onto the island before dark and set the thing up with a makeshift screen strung between two trees and with the portable generator nearby. Then Jeanne and I would return to the boat for dinner before going back after dark to run the movie. They would all be waiting anxiously, sitting in front of the screen when we arrived. As usual, "Twenty Thousand Leagues" was the big hit and there was a lot of laughing and hooting at the octopus fight scene.

John took me everywhere around the islands. On one excursion, we entered a hut on the beach in a neighboring village and there were all the elders sitting around in a circle on the matted floor. The ceremonial kava bowl sat next to the chief and his young daughter was stirring the contents. It was obvious all this was for me and I was motioned to sit cross legged in the circle with them. Kava is a strange drink, tasting and looking a little like dishwater, it has a narcotic effect on the throat. Made from the roots of a small shrub belonging to the pepper family, it has no alcohol content and can be taken in large doses without affecting your senses. What it does affect is your body, with a sort of numbness. With some ceremony, I was handed the first coconut-shell bowl and everyone watched as I took a few sips. John smiled and indicated that I was to drink the whole thing so I up-ended the bowl and downed the contents to everyone's satisfaction. The bowl was then refilled and passed around to each one in turn. When everyone had participated, it was my turn again and so it went until the big Kava bowl was empty. After a kava party, all you want to do is lie down but John and I had to get back to my waiting dinghy and cross a lagoon to the boat. Jeanne laughed when she saw the two of us arrive in a state of semi-stupor. Another evening, John asked if I would play guitar and sing for the men of his village, which I did. We gathered at one of the men's homes and sang into the evening with Susie and the other kids outside, laughing at our noise.

We enjoyed these people immensely and hated to leave but we had a schedule to meet for the first time in many months. Grant, my friend and ex-boss from the company, owned a small plantation in Fiji that they had turned into a hotel and we were invited to join them on a certain date for a week's visit. I had a hard time leaving John. He was a great friend and we had some enjoyable times together. When he found out we were leaving the following day, he came aboard with his brother and presented me with some carvings he had made and Jeanne with a beautiful tapa cloth. We were overwhelmed by their generosity. These people had so little but wanted to share with us. John and his brother were building a new boat and I had an extra outboard motor, so I gave it to them. They were very grateful. The next morning, we were preparing to leave when John came out to the boat and insisted I come to his house for a meal he was preparing. I was anxious to leave but he insisted and I told Jeanne I had to go. It was with some difficulty, I tore myself away in the afternoon to get the boat underway. There were tears streaming down his face when I left him on the beach and he stood there until we sailed down the channel and out of sight heading toward the open sea.

Suva, in the Fiji islands was a major port and an interesting one. There were a huge number of Indians there as well as the native Fijiian population. The marketplace was a panorama of color and excitement with every conceivable thing to buy from Kava to Boar's tooth jewelry. We enjoyed it and spent our time at the anchorage in front of the Royal Suva Yacht Club. They welcomed visitors and provided all kinds of entertainment in the evenings from movies to excellent barbecued steaks. After being at sea for a period of time, this was luxury we appreciated. We also had the enjoyment of meeting other cruising people on boats from all over the world. We had a week of this before sailing to the north island of "Vanua Levu" to meet Grant and his family. His place was called "Namale" and sat on a bluff overlooking tiny "Nandi Bay." We anchored in the middle of it and spent a wonderful week in the lap of luxury at his small hotel. There was entertainment provided in the evening by singers, dancers and musicians from a neighboring village, and luau's on the beach. We were thoroughly spoiled by the time our stay was over and I feared I might lose my crew to this soft life. We sailed back to Suva, a few pounds heavier from all the good food, and prepared to clear with the authorities and proceed west.

We raised anchor in Suva harbor and with a favorable wind, made our way through the pass and around the south coast of the island. The New Hebredes lay six-hundred miles to the west and we shaped our course for the island of "Efate." Five days later, we had the island in sight but darkness closed in and we hove to until morning. With all sail set the following day, we ghosted along in light air and entered the small, colorful harbor of "Vila." Our anchor went down into the coral-studded bottom just in front of a little hotel with an eating porch overhanging the water. We had come from Suva completely under sail without having to use the engine, even to enter the harbor.

The Tricolors of the French flew over one government building while the British Union Jack flew over the other. This was the only condominium government in the world and we were free to choose which one we wanted to check in with. Whichever we chose, we would be under their laws and jurisdiction as long as we were in the islands. I chose the English because of an absence of any language barrier and we settled in for a week's stay.

Much of the New Hebredes was still untouched by civilization and the home to thousands of stone-age people. We didn't know if we would make any contact with them but I wanted to see the islands, so we left Vila and started our trek through them. It was to be a lonely two-week sail from one anchorage to another on four islands.

The first evening, we anchored off some bluffs on the opposite end of Efate island. After dinner, the three of us climbed into our dinghy and rowed along the shore under the bluffs. As we rounded a point, a small wild goat was crying it's heart out up on the bluff. Soon, we saw why. The mother was stranded on a narrow ledge just above the water's edge and was trapped there. She was unable to get to her young one and it was probably long after feeding time for the little fella. We studied the situation and decided to try to help. After first putting Susie ashore on a convenient rock at the water's edge, Jeanne maneuvered the dingy close to the ledge and the trapped goat. I managed to climb from the boat onto the ledge with the intent of frightening her into jumping into the sea. She then only had to swim a dozen yards where a path led back up the bluff. As I stood on the narrow ledge, six feet above the water, I could see the animal was terrified of my presence and uncertain what to do. She was not so small, probably weighing around eighty pounds and sporting two short curved horns. Her udder was full and dripping milk so I knew she was a bit uncomfortable. I moved toward her a few steps, waving my arms and she bolted, not into the water, but straight at me. I managed to retain my spot as she brushed past me wild-eyed. This maneuver was repeated several times and I could not get her off the ledge and into the water. Finally, with a determined effort on the next charge, I managed to grab her horns and we both fell off the ledge and landed in the dinghy with Jeanne. The goat was thrashing around and bawling but I held on for dear life as Jeanne hurriedly rowed for the path. When we were close, I wrestled the animal overboard and it swam the few feet to shore and rushed up the cliffs. I was scratched up a bit but otherwise unhurt. Of course, we all felt good about our rescue of the little guy and his mama.

As we continued our journey through the islands, we hardly ever saw another human being, except, just before nightfall when the natives would come down to the water to bathe. They were very shy and if we went ashore, they would disappear into the interior. We saw their empty dwellings but never approached them. At one anchorage, there was a deserted French plantation at the head of the bay and we did our washing, using fresh water from their storage tanks. Well-used paths crossed the area but they were not used while we were there. After a week of good weather, conditions began to change and the wind increased as we worked our way down the forty-mile-long eastern side of Malekula island. I developed severe pains in my chest so we pulled into a place called "Bushman's Bay" and dropped anchor off a deserted beach. The wind remained strong for two days and I stayed in my bunk reading the Merc Manual from my medical library trying to figure out what was wrong with me. I finally decided it may have been pleurisy, an inflammation of the membrane that lines the chest and possibly caused by my experience with the goat. With two days rest, the pain was gone and we moved on toward Luganville on Espirito Santo island. After a pleasant day of great sailing in moderate wind, we coasted the town of Luganville and searched for a suitable anchorage. A mile past the town the wind began to rise, and in light rain showers we headed for a likely landing spot. By the time we arrived and anchored, the wind was blowing fresh, the bay was full of chop, and it was impossible to launch a dinghy. I let out lots of scope on the anchor chain and we went below to wait out the storm.

CHAPTER FOURTEEN

THE ISLAND OF "ESPIRITO SANTO" loomed over us and the wind howled through the rigging. Our anchor clung tenaciously to the mud bottom and chain ground against the bobstay as we swung in wide arcs with the gusts. The crew was shipbound for two days and passed the time reading, playing cards and occasionally climbing the ladder to peer out at the island and the beach a hundred yards away. Coconut palms grew almost to the water's edge and they were swaying in the wind as waves crashed on the narrow stretch of sand at their base. The sea was a caldron at the place where we would have to land our dinghy to get ashore when the wind died. This island in the southwest Pacific had meaning for me. It was the home of Bloody Mary, Nellie Frobush, Joe Cable, Bus Adams, Luther Billis, The Frenchman, and Bali Hai. Thirty-five years before, thousands of soldiers and sailors were stationed on this island as we fought our Pacific offensive in World War Two. One of them, the young Navy Lieutenant James A. Michener, was beginning his *Tales of the South Pacific*. This was the last and largest island in the New Hebredes group and our jumping-off place to a yet undetermined destination.

On the morning of the third day, the early morning sun slanted in through a porthole and awakened me from a sound sleep. I realized conditions had changed because the ship was still and riding on a quiet sea. The wind was down for the first time in three days and I stepped through the hatch on deck to view the now quiet beach and landing spot. I awakened Jeanne to come and look. We could now go ashore for the first time. We jumped into our clothes and I told Susie we were leaving for a short excursion. Jeanne made a thermos of coffee while I launched the dinghy and we headed for a likely spot to land on the beach. It felt good to be ashore and we took a path that led to a road just a short distance inland. We followed the road in the direction of "Luganville" and enjoyed the walk in the still, fresh morning. After a mile, we crossed a high bridge over a rain-swollen river and descended into the town. This had been a busy place during the war but it was quiet now with only a few businesses stretched out for a half mile along the road.

As always, we headed for the Post Office first to pick up our mail, then to the stores to find fresh food if it was available. Heavily laden with packages, we retraced our steps back to the boat in the first heat of the day to share breakfast and mail with Susie. This was our last stop in the western Pacific and we spent the next week exploring the surrounding area and trying to decide what to do. Our options were several. We could head for Torres Strait and enter the Indian Ocean for a run to Europe and an eventual circumnavigation or we could head south to Australia and spend six months waiting out the coming hurricane season. The final option was to move north and eventually to Hawaii to wait for spring before going west again. For a few days, we seriously considered the Indian Ocean and Europe but there were some problems. The Suez Canal was closed and due to be reopened before we would reach it in January, but you could never be sure. There were political problems brewing on the west coast of Africa should we decide to head for the Cape of Good Hope and that route into the Atlantic. I had a

desire to visit the Central Pacific islands that I had flown
through after the World War and the trip back to Hawaii would
open that possibility for us the following spring. After a week of
indecision, we opted for Hawaii. After all, it was home for a
change and we had seen a lot of remote islands. Considering
what eventually happened to us in the far reaches of the
Central Pacific, it was a fateful decision.

With our sights now set for Hawaii, we moved the boat
about five miles up the island to a deserted bay close to a
coconut plantation where fresh water could be obtained and
anchored for a couple of days. Susie and I made many trips in
the dinghy to the head of the bay to fill water jugs from a tap on
the plantation. There didn't seem to be anyone around so we
just helped ourselves. When the tanks were topped, we made
sail, headed for a pass through the fringing reef and set our
course for "Tarara" in the Gilbert Islands. My plan for reaching
Hawaii from this point in the Western Pacific was different
than any I had heard of before. We would sail to the Gilberts
and take on a full load of fuel. Then we would enter the
equatorial countercurrent with its light winds and easterly
current for a power run as far east as our fuel would take us.
When it was nearly exhausted, we would turn north, enter the
northeast trades and beat our way to Hawaii.

After thirteen days of great sailing, we raised the Island of
"Kuria" in the Southern Gilbert Islands. There was an island
trading vessel off-loading supplies as we approached and I
thought I might secure fuel from them and save the stop at
"Tarawa" but they departed as we arrived so I continued
sailing in closer to the island and anchored some distance off a
sand beach. We decided to rest for awhile before moving on to
Tarara but soon an outrigger approached with several men
aboard. One was wearing some kind of uniform and although
they were very friendly, we were told regulations forbade us
from landing on the Island before first clearing with the authorities at "Tarawa." I said I understood but, would it be all

73

right if we stayed at anchor for awhile? They said that wouldn't violate the regulations and, with friendly waves, left for the beach. It wasn't long before the same group was again pulling up to our boat in the outrigger. This time, the uniform was gone and the canoe was filled with fresh fruit and drinking coconuts. We invited them aboard and they enjoyed inspecting the boat and allowing us to return their hospitality. Late in the afternoon, we said our good-byes and left for an overnight run to Tarawa.

This little island in the Gilberts, only two miles long and one-half mile wide, was the scene of one of the first and bloodiest battles of the Pacific during World War Two. As I approached the docks at the end of a long fairway, I was well aware that hundreds of men died in the waters surrounding me, trying to reach the same spot I was now heading for. The din and destruction of battle had long since faded from memory but some of the reminders of war were still to be seen. Large coastal guns faced seaward and concrete bunkers pocked with bullet holes still stood among palm trees in the middle of the island. There was quite a dense population for the size of the atoll and a group gathered on the concrete dock to greet us as we moved alongside. A Chinese man ran the fuel dump and arranged to deliver diesel fuel to us the next day while a local British couple invited us to dinner at their home. Without a prearranged Visa for this remote outpost, we were limited to a three-day stay but that suited our purpose. The British ruled these islands for years until they were taken over by the Japanese during the war. They were now back in the hands of the British trained Gilbertese who had a healthy respect for a strict interpretation of the rules. With this in mind, we sailed away shortly before our allotted time was up.

With fuel tanks loaded to capacity, we plowed into the equatorial countercurrent and headed east under power and sail for the long run to Hawaii. We were veterans of the Pacific now and distances meant very little to us. We had full confidence in ourselves and our vessel and would point her any-where in the world we wanted to go without hesitation. The countercurrent gave us an extra push of up to one extra nautical mile every hour and we made long runs every twenty-four hours for the next two weeks. The weather was typical of the doldrums with light winds, overcast skies and some rain show-ers. Susie celebrated her birthday at sea for the second time and we settled into our shipboard routine as the engine pushed us eastward and the days passed. It was more work for us because the wind vane wouldn't perform under power and we had to stand watches at the helm.

When we were nearing the end of our fuel supply, I judged us to be just far enough east to make Hawaii on a starboard tack. We hardened up on the sheets and beat into the Northeast Tradewind. As we did so, the current and leeway was setting us to the west and our progress was slowed to about four knots as we moved north, hard on the wind. I wished I had taken on another barrel of fuel at Tarawa but it was too late to worry about it and I watched our progress taking us west of the main islands of Hawaii. Our desired destination was Honolulu but when we reached the latitude of this island, we were a hundred miles west of it with no way to head into the teeth of the Northeast Trades to reach it. We continued on northward for another night and early the following morning I had the small island of "Niihau," which is only a large volcanic rock, dead ahead of us. With light winds, we worked our way into the lee of the island of Kauai and with our last remaining fuel, powered to the little town of Port Allen on the south coast. We were thirty-eight days out of Espirito Santo in the New Hebredes with only a forty-eight hour stop at Tarawa. We were also twelve-thousand miles out of San Francisco with almost a year of steady sailing under our belts. Within a few days, "Evening Star" was tied up at the Hawaii Yacht Club in Honolulu with the crew enjoying the many pleasures of Waikiki Beach. It was good to be home.

CHAPTER FIFTEEN

Two weeks after returning to Hawaii, I had a chance to earn a little extra money. A warm sun bore into my bare back as I worked on deck. The splice was going slowly because of the salt hardened line and I pushed it aside to rest my complaining fingers. A familiar figure was moving across the grass below the Yacht Club veranda toward the boat and I watched him thread his way around the many sails stretched out to dry on the hot grass. I acknowledged his wave and waited while he walked the boarding plank and stretched out against a sail bag just under the deck awning.

"Don" was a friend of many years and he came right to the point. "I came to offer you a job if you want it. I just had a call from a man on the Big Island who had his boat in our shipyard a short time ago. He's a wealthy young buck from the mainland with a sixty-five-foot motorsailor that he wants to take to Tahiti. It seems he started the trip himself a week ago and turned around only one day south of the Island in rough waters. His crew of four is restless and eating all the provisions and he can't find anyone he's willing to trust the boat with. He's asked me to do the job but I can't get away right now so I told him I would talk to you. Any interest?"

I started to say no, but then thought better of it considering it had been almost two years since I had seen any earnings. Besides needing the money, I thought it might be interesting to sail a larger boat with a full crew for a change. I knew my friends would keep a weather eye on my boat and family while I was gone so I told him to sign me on.

The middle-aged skipper who climbed aboard the commuter plane in Honolulu the next morning was thin and physically hardened from many months at sea. From my vantage point in the aircraft, I could see a familiar little ship at anchor, now on Keehi Lagoon, as the plane climbed into the fresh Hawaiian morning heading for the Big Island of Hawaii. The Kona coast looked like the back side of the moon as the plane approached the runway an hour later. It looked like we were landing on the black jagged surface of a lava field but at the last minute before touchdown, a ribbon of concrete appeared under the wheels. A thin young man in his middle thirties, dressed like a flower child and sporting a large red beard, was waiting for me at the gate. We had a danish and coffee before heading for his ship.

She sat quietly, moored to a dirt bank, in the small harbor just up the island from Kona. There was some activity on the aft deck and a couple of young men poled an open boat toward us. I knew all eyes were on me but mine were on the ship itself. It looked reasonably well maintained as I took in the whole of her decks and rigging. The name that graced her stern meant nothing to me but something told me I had known her before in other times and with another name, possibly when I worked in the shipyard in Newport Beach over twenty years before. I was introduced to the crew and we almost immediately got under way for Kona to take on water.

That evening, darkness descended on the harbor quite suddenly and with it came a little wind. We were then anchored off the main pier with two stern lines leading to the dock to hold us close. Small waves were beginning to slap against the pilings only twenty feet away and I took up a few notches on the anchor windlass before going below for a sandwich and cold beer. I had set a sailing time for 2200 hours and the ship was quiet while the owner and crew were ashore doing last minute things. The owner and his girlfriend were going to see us off, then fly to Tahiti to await our arrival. I had a couple of hours to prowl the vessel and get a feel for her gear, potential problems and complexities. I knew the potential problems on an old girl like her would be well hidden and only show up on a black night amid lots of wind and chaos. All I really was looking for was an indication of strength and soundness in rigging and gear. The fact that this lady was built in 1925 when builders knew and cared about such things was comforting.

I thought about my crew. When I arrived that morning there were four of them, three young men and a girl who was to do the cooking. Now there were three, the girl having decided to quit the ship. I had learned a little about the men during the afternoon from the owner and my own observations. They were all young, in their very early twenties, and part of the hoard of young people then wandering around the islands, sleeping in hostels and surviving on very little money. A trip to Tahiti with all expenses paid was an attractive offer to this group until they got their first taste of the sea on the aborted one-day trip south of the island. It seemed they actually had three days at sea because after turning around one day into the voyage, it took them two days to struggle back against wind and seas to the lee of the island. They evidently were all a bit shaken by the experience but evidently had decided to stay with the ship for another try. A trip to Tahiti has always been a powerful magnet for young men, this group especially, with no money in their jeans.

They were a close-knit threesome and were already viewing me with skepticism. I was not accorded any degree of welcome and their attitude even bordered on rudeness when I arrived aboard that morning. I ignored them most of the day as

I familiarized myself with the ship. It was evident there was quite a generation gap or two between us. I represented an authority figure and this generation openly proclaimed on their bumper stickers, "question authority." The three were very diverse in character. My biggest problem, I had already determined, was "Jeff." He was a husky pugnacious guy of medium height and obviously, the leader of the three. He was the only one with some sailing experience on small boats and made no bones about his contempt of my being brought aboard. I think he had a friend with some experience who they hoped would be given the job. Maybe he also thought I was too old for this rigorous life and the sea belonged to younger men like himself. He had not made any remarks openly to me but just a sly smile and a wink to his friends when I asked him to do some chore. I knew he would be my problem but he was strong and I needed him.

James was tall and thin and the better educated of the three. I liked his easygoing demeanor and I even sensed a willingness to learn but, of course, he had his loyalty to his leader and I hadn't tried to invade their shell in our short relationship. "Lee" was the youngest of the trio, sandy-haired and quiet, with seemingly not much energy or enthusiasm. He just liked to hang out with his friends and laugh at their jokes. He was frequently the butt of the jokes and took it good-naturedly. I would have to weld them into a responsible crew if we were to get the vessel safely to Tahiti. Sailing a ship of this size is no joke and could turn into a nightmare and even a killer if not handled properly. There was no time to worry about that. I knew the wind was freshening from the increased motion of the boat so I finished my beer and went topside.

We were in relatively shallow water and the vessel was pitching a bit and hauling hard against her anchor chain on the bow. There was slack in our stern lines and only about twelve feet separated us from the concrete dock. Our tender was banging against the pilings and I surveyed the town and entrance to the dock to see if my crew were on their way back. The wind was up and a few drops of rain beginning to fall. Realizing we could be in a precarious situation if our anchor dragged, I stepped into the wheelhouse and started both engines. When I had them both turning, I looked around to see my crew along with the owner and his girlfriend, running down the dock toward the boat. I yelled above the noise of the engine and wind for the crew to come aboard and for the owner to stand by to cast off our lines. He kept trying to question me about something but I couldn't hear him. When the guys were aboard, I told them to haul the tender aboard as quickly as possible. When it was on deck, I sent Jeff and Lee into the bows to stand by the windlass and James aft to stand by our stern lines. The "Red Beard" was trying to tell me something but I motioned him to let go the stern lines and as loud as I could yell, "See you in Tahiti in three weeks." He nodded and cast us off. I signalled Jeff with both thumbs up to start the anchor in and eased the vessel away from the dock. In a few minutes, the rain shower obscured the town as we slowly made our way straight ahead into the night and deep water.

I sent my crew below to get into dry clothes as I studied the chart and plotted a course to keep us safely offshore but still in the protected lee of the island. It was close to midnight when the crew assembled in the wheelhouse. Their bravado was gone and in the blackness, I could sense their apprehension about what was ahead. The biggest thing they feared was moving out of the lee of the land into those big seas that awaited us just beyond. I would have preferred to raise sail and be on our way but my better judgement told me to hove to until daylight. I was aware that I not only had an inexperienced crew but that I wasn't that familiar with the ship myself. They were visibly relieved when I suggested they get some sleep. "We'll set the watches and get underway at first light."

CHAPTER SIXTEEN

I DOZED IN THE WHEELHOUSE UNTIL DAWN, then woke the crew and started a pot of coffee on the galley range. When we assembled in the wheelhouse, I made my little speech.

"Our objective is to get this vessel to Tahiti safely with all of us still aboard and in good health. A few things to remember: If you happen to go overboard at night, the chances of you ever getting back aboard are slim. If you go overboard and none of the rest of us see it happen, the chances are zero. If you go overboard in heavy weather, even if we do see it happen, your chances are nil. The message here is—just don't go overboard. The best way to prevent this is to always be alert and aware of the motion of the boat when on deck. The old rule of one hand for the ship and one for yourself is a good one. One rule I insist upon without exception is: never go on deck at night without waking one of your shipmates and never fail to wake me if you see a light of any kind at night. One of the greatest hazards at sea is being run down by a large vessel. Feel free to wake me at any time for anything. We will all stand wheel watches around the clock. I'll take the 6 to 9. Lee, you will have the 9 to 12. Jeff the 12 to 3 and James, the 3 to 6. When on watch, I'll expect you to concentrate on steering a good course. That means no reading or other activity. Just steer and keep a good lookout, not just ahead of the ship, but also astern. Any questions?"

Jeff spoke up. "Yeah, how about cooking?"

"Good question. I should have covered that. You guys will have to share the cooking. Breakfast will be at 1100 and the evening meal at 1800. How you share the chore is up to you but I do want the galley cleaned after every meal and the ship kept clean. Snacks any other time are up to you and I may help out on a breakfast now and then. My pancakes are famous all over the Pacific. Now, lets get this vessel underway for Tahiti. Lee, you stand by the wheel and the rest of us will get us under sail."

We worked for half an hour getting all sail up and the sun was just coming up as the ship moved off slowly south toward the end of the island. It was a good feeling to have two healthy young men doing the heavy work hauling halyards and sheets. On my own vessel, this work was reserved for me. As the sun climbed higher in the eastern sky, we were reaching into increasing seas away from the lee of the island and I took the wheel to get the feel of the ship. At 0900, she was steadied down on course and Lee took over on his first watch. I helped him get the feel of steering a compass course before going below for a breakfast snack.

The first day went smoothly with all of us catching as many naps as we could to make up for the lack of sleep the previous night. With the wind fresh, we were rolling southward at a good clip. I fixed a drink and took over the wheel at 1800. My crew went below to fix dinner and I enjoyed having the wheelhouse to myself. They had all been clustered up there most of the day getting their sea legs and were pretty quiet. Getting over the discomfort of the first couple of days at sea is always difficult and they were, of course, thinking it was going to be that way for the whole long hard trip. I knew their depression would disappear in a day or so but you couldn't tell them that. In another half hour, James came up with a tray for me. It contained a bowl of soup and some bread and butter. He said, "It's pretty rough

82

in the galley, so we're not having much tonight." I started to go along with that but decided it better not to.

"James, It's not going to get any easier. We need a good meal under our belts and you have to learn to function at sea in all kinds of conditions. You'll just have to go below, plant your feet in that galley and get us a dinner going. We should have at least some meat and potatoes and we're going to have a solid meal every night no matter how rough it gets. Believe me, it will get easier."

He wasn't too happy with that response but said, "OK We've already eaten but I'll fix you something."

With that, he disappeared down the hatchway and I tackled the soup. I could imagine the conversation and name calling when he returned to his buddies but I had to establish control early with this group or I never would.

I received my dinner and sullen looks from all of them when they finally came up with it. Lee took the helm at 2100 and I stayed with him awhile before going below for a few hours sleep. I planned to spend a little time on each of their watches this first night and I was weary from lack of sleep myself. My mental alarm clock got me up a few hours later and I stumbled topside to see James at the wheel and the other two rolled up in blankets along the bulkhead of the small wheelhouse.

"James, what are you doing on watch? I thought I assigned the 12 to 3 to Jeff."

"Well, he was a little tired and I wasn't, so we switched."

"James, it's no big deal tonight but, from now on, I need to know when you want to make a change. I assign these watches for a reason and why is everybody sleeping up here?" He admitted they were all a little queasy down below and thought they would try it up here. I walked over to the nearest form and bumped it with my toe. It was Jeff and he raised up glaring at me. "Jeff, I don't like anyone underfoot in the wheelhouse at night. Either sleep below or on the aft deck." I didn't wait for an answer and just walked over to James at the wheel and waited for the two of them to move their bedrolls out. I hated to be harsh with them so early in our relationship but I needed some discipline from three individuals who, it seemed, had not been exposed to much of it. I alone knew of the dangers and seriousness of managing a ship like this with an inexperienced crew so I decided to play it tough. They really hadn't given me any slack to play it differently, so far. I secretly hoped they would come around as the voyage progressed but I wasn't too optimistic. It looked like it was going to be a lonely existence for me the next few weeks and I scanned the meager library in the master cabin when I went below. There was *The Wake of the Red Witch*. I plowed into it for company.

The second night out, the wind freshened and we were boiling down big seas with the bows depressed in the troughs and white phosphorescent waves curling off our beam. I could sense my crew's anxiety as we gathered in the wheelhouse to plan strategy. I decided to bring the massive mainsail down instead of trying to reef it and that presented a danger. Instead of a gallows to drop the main boom in, there was only a boom crutch on top of the house. Trying to get that heavy spar into the crutch on a rough night would have been dangerous. It could easily knock a man overboard or break a leg if it got out of control, so I decided to let it rest on deck with lashings until morning. Looking out on that darkened deck with spray flying across it, Jeff asked the question. "Who do you want on deck?" I knew he didn't expect me to go out. The owner-skipper didn't, and they were surprised to learn I was even going to stand a wheel watch. I knocked the ashes out of my pipe and said, casually, "This is too important a job to turn over to a bunch of amateurs. You and I and James will do the honors and Lee will take the helm." I knew he was relieved.

When we worked our way out into the night and gathered at the foot of the mainmast, I gave them a bit of advice. "Don't hurry. We'll take our time and down her inch by inch if we have to. Just watch your footing."

As we ran off before the wind, it took the strength of all three of us twenty minutes to get that big piece of canvas down, James on the main halyard winch and Jeff and I fighting to control the sail as it came down. It was a stubborn job until we had it blanketed somewhat by the mizzen, but then it gave way to our efforts and soon covered the deck. Getting it furled and held with gaskets was the toughest job, and we were all sweating profusely when it was done and the boom lashed. The guys had performed well and I purposely remained on deck enjoying watching the vessel slash through the cresting seas. Once the fear of working on a heaving deck is behind you, it leaves a feeling of strength and I wanted these guys to feel it. I think, for the first time they realized we could handle anything that needed doing aboard the ship, and I could sense their feeling of confidence. The easy camaraderie they shared with me when we went back to the wheelhouse for coffee was a small victory, and I hoped, maybe even a breakthrough in our relationship.

In five days, we stormed through the last of the northeast trades and entered the equatorial countercurrent and the doldrums. The weather clouded over and intermittent rain showers were frequent. We were constantly changing sails and course and it was hard work in foul weather gear most of the time. The guys were learning that sailing was more than the romantic notion they thought it to be. My experience so far with the vessel told me she was not a good windward passagemaker and there would be a lot of that on the final run to Tahiti.

We cranked up the two big diesels and ran east in the countercurrent for two days. James turned out to be a good engine-room man, checking oil and keeping the bilges pumped. We had two problems down there. First, we were taking water through the shaft bearings and also had a leak in the engine's freshwater cooling system. We couldn't stop either of them so it took regular pumping of the bilges and James watched it closely. After a day, the main bilge pump burned out so we found a portable gasoline pump aboard that had good capacity. It was supposed to be for topside use in washing down the decks but we put it to use in the engine room. The only problem was the carbon monoxide it emitted from the exhaust and James struggled to get the small engine running when needed, without being overcome by fumes before he could exit the tight space down there. He took the responsibility though and I didn't have to worry about it.

My crew was beginning to shape up well. Jeff was my deck mate, James handled the machinery and Lee became a pretty good cook. When we praised his culinary skills, he worked all the harder to earn our respect, even making fresh bread and biscuits. After the first week, I had a respectable working relationship with the crew although I was still not accepted in their inner circle. Things remained like this for the rest of the voyage and I was satisfied, feeling a stronger control over the ship with this state of affairs.

After gaining some easting under power, we again turned south and entered the Southeast Tradewinds. These winds were lighter and our progress slowed but the weather was pleasant and the guys enjoyed fishing off the stern and sun-bathing on deck. They were really into the voyage now and enjoying the seaman's life. I couldn't help but think they were a different group from the kids I had started with. They were beginning to realize that each shouldered a heavy responsibility for the ship and everyone aboard. Jeff followed the navigation procedures closely and I encouraged him to learn. I let them have their camaraderie and time alone and I spent long hours in my cabin reading. I just wanted to get the job over with, pick up my money and get back to my family and boat. There was only one flight a week out of Tahiti for Honolulu by way of Samoa and our progress was such that I would make it with a day to spare without having to spend an extra week waiting for the next one.

The last ten days went without incident until we were within a couple of hundred miles of our destination. Our course would take us by the lee shore of "Tetiaroa" island less than forty miles north of Tahiti but the wind shifted and we were close hauled trying to stay a safe distance off the atoll. With heavy rain showers and low visibility, we spent an uneasy night on watch as we charged past the little island. With the morning came continued unsettled weather and with my eye on that plane departure the following day, we motorsailed until almost noon. By then, we had fair weather again and the big beautiful mountains of Tahiti in view off our bow.

It was another satisfying landfall for me but my crew was excited and couldn't take their eyes off the green shape of Tahiti and Moorea as we approached the islands. We were back under sail and charged through the pass into Papeete harbor. As we rounded up into the wind to douse our sails, the harbor pilot came alongside and led us to the quarantine dock and customs office. "Red Beard" was there to meet us. He had been watching that pass for several days awaiting our arrival and probably wondering if he would ever see his vessel again. After the formalities were completed, we moved the ship over to the waterfront below the town and with bow anchor set, backed in to the quay, Tahiti style. Interested onlookers from the grassy bank took our stern lines and the voyage was done.

Red Beard slipped the boys a ten-spot and sent them across the road for hamburgers and ice cream while he inspected the boat and questioned me about the trip. When they returned, we set them to cleaning up the ship while we went to the airport to arrange for my flight and then to his hotel. He promised to take the crew out for dinner that evening and I knew they were eagerly awaiting a first big night out in Papeete. My flight was early the following morning and he and I sat by the pool talking.

By early evening, we returned to the boat and the guys were already cleaned up and ready for the big evening. They all had a beer on the afterdeck while I packed my gear, took a shower and changed clothes. It was sundown when we started off across the grass toward town. Red Beard said the best place to eat was the one close to the boat where my crew had bought hamburgers earlier in the day and he led us that way. I really didn't care but I knew the guys were expecting something a little more exciting for their night out. Dinner was hamburgers again and I sensed our host wanted to be rid of us as soon as he could get away. The big evening was becoming less and less likely to happen. After dinner, we walked the length of the waterfront looking at the other boats tied up from all over the world and ended up back at our vessel. Red Beard made some excuse that he would have to leave, then instructed his crew what he expected them to do on the boat the following day. With that, he departed, leaving a very disappointed group of young men sitting on the afterdeck of the boat in the most exciting island town in the Pacific with no money in their pockets. I fixed a drink and went below to finish packing. I had to be up very early the next morning to clear customs and catch my flight and, being tired from the voyage, I was looking forward to a relaxing evening.

I went on deck a while later, thinking about a walk around town before turning in and spotted the crew lying under a tree on the grass. I could invite them to go with me but I knew it wasn't a very exciting prospect. I felt sorry for them. They had earned a better deal so I made a quick decision and a change of plans. I strolled over casually and said, "Guys, I'm going out for a drink and see what's going on in this town. You're welcome to come along. My treat."

Gloom turned to smiles as they jumped to their feet and I led the way to the biggest and noisiest saloon on the waterfront. It was full of sailors, tourists and island girls dressed in their finest. There were three bars strung around the cavernous building and a loud band in full swing. This was the Tahiti these guys had looked forward to seeing and they were in great spirits, taking it all in. When I bought the first round of drinks, it was evident the forty dollars I had on me wouldn't go very far so I excused myself and headed for one of the bar managers. I told him I had a party to entertain and would he accept a credit card. He said no, cash only, but I could go next door to the hotel. They owned the bar.

I went next door, found the manager and explained the situation. He took my credit card, had me sign a slip and wrote a note to the bar manager. When I returned to my young friends, I told them, "You did a hell of a job on the trip down and I appreciate it. The night's on me so drink up and enjoy." For the rest of the evening, we put away all the beer we could drink and danced with the girls until the wee hours. It took James and I both to help Lee back to the boat. I went to bed knowing I had only a few hours to sleep but I could catch up on that on the long flight home.

I was up early and the ship was quiet. I knew the sun would be well up before the guys stirred so I shouldered my things and started up the plank to shore. As I reached the top, a voice from the deck called. "Hey Skipper!" That was the first time I had been addressed as such and I turned to see Jeff, standing barefooted in his shorts, on the afterdeck. I stopped, un-shouldered my load and he came up the plank with hand outstretched. We shook hands and he said, "Bill, I just wanted to say good-bye and to tell you we didn't mean to give you such a hard time on the boat. "What I mean is—We wouldn't have made it without you and I—well—we all learned a lot from you. What I mean is—" He was stumbling for words and I cut him short.

"Jeff, I couldn't have made it without you. Good luck and I hope you enjoy your stay down here. If things don't work out with Red Beard, there are plenty of other vessels here always looking for crew. They could do a lot worse than you guys." With that, I shouldered my gear and without looking back, headed across the grass for the road. Maybe I helped these guys a little on that tough road through young manhood. I never saw them again.

CHAPTER SEVENTEEN

BACK IN HAWAII WITH A FEW EXTRA DOLLARS in my jeans, I rejoined the family and "Evening Star," riding at anchor on Keehi Lagoon. The plan was to enjoy ourselves in Hawaii through Christmas and then head west to the Marshall and Caroline Islands. From there, I had a rough itinerary and timetable that would take us to Europe and an eventual circumnavigation of the world. The past two years had been a wonderful experience for us, visiting people and places in remote parts of the Pacific.

The Hawaiian Islands had changed dramatically since I first viewed them thirty years earlier as a young Navy man. They captured my soul then and changed my destiny for a lifetime. Before I boarded a Navy transport ship for the voyage to Honolulu, my greatest ambition was to be a rancher in the high country of Colorado or Montana raising horses and cattle. After my stint in the Navy in the Pacific, I was forever after a seaman with salt water in my blood. Honolulu in those days, right after World War Two, was relatively quiet. There were only two main hotels on Waikiki Beach, the Royal Hawaiian and the Moana, and only the more wealthy segment of society visited them. They arrived by ship and it was a grand event when the

"Lurline" docked under the big clock tower in downtown Honolulu. Bands were playing and the smell of flower leis was in the air along with the excitement of something special. The Aloha spirit was real and everything slowed down to Hawaiian time. The music was ukuleles, guitars and the dance was "Hula" with the girls as graceful as the Island palms swaying in the breeze.

Kalakaua Avenue, the main road that wound through Waikiki, was a place to stroll on Sunday afternoons with flower sellers on every corner and the scent of their blossoms was in the air. It was a magical place that I missed tremendously when I was shipped home in 1952. By the time I saw it again in the sixties, it was a completely different place and had become a tourist mecca with easy access from the mainland by jet aircraft. It remains so today but it still has a certain charm that I enjoy every time I visit.

We now settled in for our time in the islands. You could no longer anchor in Ala Wai Harbor in Waikiki and it was too crowded to allow visiting boats more than a few weeks there. The other available anchorage was Keehi Lagoon, near the airport. It was not a convenient place to be, far removed from easy access to Waikiki and the beaches, but there were many itinerant vessels like ourselves anchored there and we made some friends. My old friend, Ken Murray, was a frequent companion and a great help to us when we needed transportation or information about anything. He knew the islands like the back of his hand and we enjoyed his company.

In early November, an unfortunate incident happened. Jeanne, Susie and I were playing cards in the chartroom when a shadow fell over the sunny interior of the boat and we looked up to see a huge barge drifting into our port side. It had gotten away from the tug that was handling it and drifted into the anchorage. We rushed on deck to the sound of splintering wood and grinding metal. When the thing was pushed away from us, I surveyed the damage: broken bowsprit and yardarm, crushed rubrail and stanchons, torn running rigging and general loss of paint. The boat that was ready to go to sea only a few minutes ago, was now a mess. Our work was cut out for us if we wanted to continue our voyage on schedule.

The barge was owned by one of the largest companies in the islands and their surveyor came aboard to assess the damage. We both agreed on a sum of $7,500.00 dollars in damages and I requested a cash settlement to handle my own repairs. They agreed, but after several weeks went by with no check, I pressed them for action. They said it took time for their insurance company to pay and to be patient. We were, for another few weeks; then in desperation, I went to an attorney. He wrote a letter to the shipping company on my behalf stating that our long worked-for plans were in jeopardy if we didn't receive payment from them immediately. Again, I waited. After another week went by, I told the attorney to set a deadline of the following Friday or we would file suit for damages that included loss of our planned voyage. When I called him on Friday morning, he said the company would have a check for us the following Monday. I was through being put off so I told him I would be in his office before 5:00 PM that day for a check. If it was not forthcoming, I would not accept the damage settlement we had formerly agreed upon. I guess they decided I was serious. I was sitting in his outer office at 5:00 when my attorney walked in from the shipping company offices across the street. He had my check in hand.

My friend, Don Anderson, already had repairs under way. Don is a master shipright and when he finished the new bowsprit and other woodwork, it looked like new again. I had a new yardarm shipped in from the mainland and deposited on the dock at Keehi Lagoon. We pushed it into the water and floated it out to the boat where I lifted it aboard with block and tackle. After fitting the hardware and running rigging, we hauled it up the mainmast and were ready for sea again.

Christmas had come and gone and Susie was on the mainland visiting her mother and friends.

Jeanne and I were getting anxious to resume our travels and the Central Pacific Islands would be our next challenge. This was the vast Trust Territories of the United States, set up by the United Nations after the war. Until recently, no one had been allowed to visit some of these islands unless on government business. The Trust Territories included the Marshall Islands, the Carolines and the Marianas, the heart of Micronesia. I was curious to see what they were like thirty years after the war and had written for the required permission to sail there. When Susie returned from the mainland, we provisioned the ship and prepared to leave.

Jeanne gathered laundry that was hanging in the rigging to dry. It was almost noon and the tide had turned seaward. A friend in a dinghy nearby was cleaning the hull of his vessel and I asked if he would play tug for me and help push the bow of our boat around into the tidal stream when I raised the anchor. It would prevent us from having to start the engine and heat up the boat. He started his outboard and came over. With no other fanfare, we hauled anchor, set the mainsail and drifted into the tidal stream for the run through the pass to sea. We were outbound around the world but fate is always the hunter.

CHAPTER EIGHTEEN

AFTER ALMOST FIVE MONTHS IN HAWAII living the soft life, our sea legs were shaky. We felt it when we cleared the lee of the island and entered the big swells, spawned in the North Pacific winter and now rolling in off our starboard quarter. The one most affected was our newest crewmember, "Sinbad." He was a little half-Siamese black cat that needed a family and we had been seduced by his need for a home. For a short while, he hunched in the cockpit well, heaving his little insides out and hating us for adopting him. We were all a little unsteady for a day but glad to be at sea and eager for a new landfall. We rolled on through the mid-Pacific and passed the only piece of land between Hawaii and the Marshall Islands. Tiny "Johnston" Island lay in our path and we saw a few lights in the distance as we passed it in the night. I had landed there many times on my Navy flights across the Pacific. Seventeen days out of Honolulu, we raised the island of "Majuro" in the southern Marshalls, just before sunset. It was a race to reach the pass into the atoll before dark but we made it in the last light of day and anchored off a deserted little palm-covered motu inside the lagoon. Another two thousand miles of ocean under our keel. A piece of cake.

I awoke in the morning and gazed upon a beautiful green island with a wide, completely clean and deserted white sand beach. The girls couldn't wait to set foot on it so I launched the dinghy and took them in. Our official entry into the Trust Territory could wait a few more hours. Thinking Sinbad would appreciate setting foot on all that sand, I took him in also but he was terrified when we set him ashore. He had already become a true "boat cat" and I took him back to his home.

A few hours later, we moved fifteen miles to the east end of Majuro atoll where the main town stretched a mile or more along a crescent- shaped island. In the southeast corner of the lagoon, we anchored in front of a small hotel. After landing our dinghy on the beach in front of it, we walked to the other end of town to present our papers to the authorities. The walk was a chance to see what the Trust Territory towns were going to be like. The houses were usually rusting one story affairs made of odd sizes of corrugated tin. I suspect a lot of it was scrap materials left behind by our military. Most of the people we met seemed to be too preoccupied to be very cordial and there was a slight sense of indifference and possibly some distrust in their demeanor. We were to learn a lot more about the people and their lives and problems in the next few months. For now, we settled in for a few weeks of island living. The water at our anchorage was crystal clear and after a few days, we began to meet people and make friends.

We were the only private vessel visiting the island so, eventually, the small American community of government employees sought us out and we became acquainted. Susie made friends with the kids and we were invited to their homes for Sunday barbecues and volley ball games. One guest at the hotel was a large friendly Texan from El Paso, visiting the islands on business with his wife. We became friends with Bob Jones and through him, we met Oscar De Brum, the Marshallese District Administrator of all the Marshall Islands. He and his wife spoke good English and were both open and friendly people. We were entertained in their home and had them out to the boat on several occasions. Oscar and Bob were interested in Celestial navigation so I started a little class for them aboard the boat and loaned Oscar a spare sextant to practice with.

After a few weeks, we were ready to move on but Jeanne received a letter from her family saying her father was very ill. We delayed our departure and she caught the next plane for home. Air Micronesia was a branch of Continental Airlines and made a flight through this part of the Pacific once a week. It was the only link with the outside world by air. Susie and I hated to see her go but we settled in to await her return. Our new friends invited us out a lot for activities and we made a side trip on a supply boat to the neighboring island of "Arno." It was a diving camp and we spent the night in a tent and dove in the clear waters of the lagoon. The next day, a small inter-island seaplane landed at the camp and gave us a ride back to Majaro. It was a fun experience flying low over the atoll and seeing "Evening Star" at anchor in the lagoon riding like a swan on turquoise water.

We didn't know when Jeanne would return so we met the plane each week to see if she was on it. After a couple of weeks, she stepped off the flight and rejoined the crew. For a few nights after her return, we repaid our friend's hospitality with dinners aboard the boat and then prepared to leave for the Caroline Islands, eight-hundred miles to the west. I planned to make one stop at the tiny Island of "Kusaie," located midway between the Marshalls and Ponape in the Carolines. After clearing with the authorities, we sailed back down the atoll to the peaceful motu next to the pass and anchored for another night, enjoying the scenery and diving off that beautiful beach.

We were underway the following morning, and at dawn on our fourth day at sea we raised the high mountainous island of Kusaie, dead ahead. As we approached, it completely disappeared in a massive rain shower and we didn't see it again until we were almost at the entrance of "Lele" harbor. Off the beaten track in the Central Pacific, this island was the lair of the pirate "Bully Hayes" in the 1800s. His ship was sunk in a storm while anchored in a small bay on the end of the island. We dropped anchor in "Lele" harbor close to one other boat up from New Guinea with a single man aboard. The compact town of rusty one-story dwellings and stores was only a few hundred yards long with one dirt road down the middle of it. A sunken steel barge on the shore in the middle of town served as a dock and immediately behind the buildings was the heavy green growth of the island. It had the appearance of a shantytown one might see in the poorer section of any major city, only the setting was one of tropical beauty. We made friends with our neighboring boat and went ashore to check in. Within a short time ashore, we met the few Americans on the island including Marvin Krebs, the District Administer. He took us to his home to meet his family and served tea. Visitors were few and far between out here and they seemed to enjoy the company. We learned that the U. S. government poured over a hundred thousand dollars a month into the island to pay salaries of people on the government payroll who had practically nothing to do. It was a form of welfare that had immobilized the local population. This was a fertile island that fed a large garrison of Japanese during their occupation of the island, but now, almost nothing was grown. We could not obtain fresh vegetables at the stores and it was sad to see such a state of apathy among the people. This Micronesian culture had been a rich one with a proud heritage for centuries, but it was evident that colonial rule by foreign elements including our own had taken it's toll. We met Peace Corps volunteers on the island who were trying to revitalize the spirit of the people but with little success. What they seemed to be lacking was a solid economy and sense of purpose. We didn't particularly enjoy our stay. Being close to the equator and out of the tradewinds much of the time, it was wet with frequent rain showers and the water around the anchorage was not clear because of the runoff. After ten days, we set sail and headed west for Ponape. There, we were to connect with Grant and another couple from Seattle, Dan and Ellen Blom. They were going to join us on the boat for a few weeks of sailing and we looked forward to the rendezvous.

At noon on our third day out of Kusaie, we passed the small island of "Mokil," about eighty miles east of Ponape. The wind freshened at nightfall with a lot of rain and, after dinner, I slept for a few hours while Jeanne and Susie tended the ship. When they retreated to their bunks at midnight, I took over and watched the weather closely for any increase in wind that would necessitate a reduction in sail. The wind was fresh and shifting direction frequently so I was constantly tending the sheets and adjusting the steering vane. An hour before daylight, the wind was up and it was raining hard. I wanted to reduce sail but was reluctant to get my crew up in that weather before daylight. I was also very tired so I decided to wait. About 0430, I went below, fixed a pot of tea and settled down in the warmth of the chartroom. I must have dozed.

The rush of fast water and the unusual motion of the boat brought me instantly awake and on my feet. With a sick dread in the pit of my stomach, I rushed for the hatch and threw it open. We were scraping along the surface of a coral reef. I hung on as the boat ground to a halt, careened slightly and settled into a fifteen degree list to port. Jeanne and Susie rushed through the cabin, startled and frightened. The events of those few moments were to change the course of my life.

PART THREE
Shipwreck

CHAPTER NINETEEN

THE FEELING OF SHOCK AND SELF-INCRIMINATION passed quickly. I just didn't have the time for it and I forced myself to concentrate on an assessment of our situation. The keel of the boat rested on the hard surface of a reef about two hundred feet from the edge in four feet of water. Since the boat normally draws seven feet, we were heeled over but still floating on our bilge. We had sailed full standing over the reef at high tide.

It was hard work on the sloping deck but the first necessity was to get the big squaresail and raffee down and stowed on deck. That took the strain off the boat and rigging so we could concentrate on other things. It appeared we were in no immediate danger and had plenty of time. There was no rough water after it passed over the reef so that eliminated the possibility of the boat breaking up or ourselves being washed away. The huge squall that put us over the reef had moved on and soon after first light, it was a very quiet morning. The rain-washed mountainous island loomed over us less than a mile away and there was no sign of habitation anywhere. Thus, completely marooned and alone on an offshore reef, we quietly went to work.

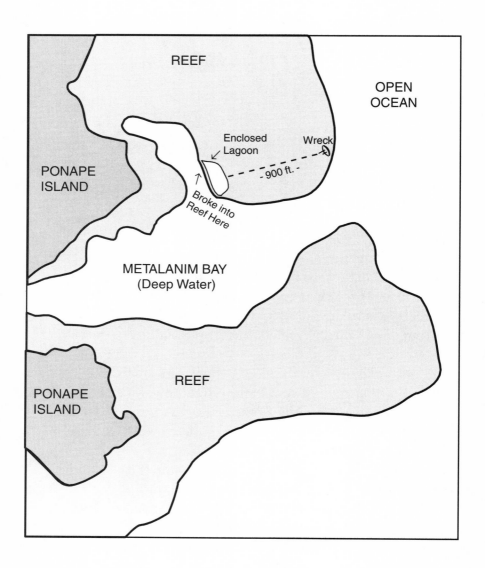

The boat was put in order both below and topsides with everything stowed and lashed down. As far as I could tell, there didn't seem to be any real damage to the old girl at all. She had been lifted on a big swell, all fifty thousand pounds of her, over the reef and gently placed on it as a baby would be placed in a crib. When we were ready to leave her to seek help, she was as neat and well stowed as if we had entered a harbor in the smartest fashion. We launched the hard dinghy, attached a small outboard to it and tied it alongside. The slow process of inflating the twelve-foot rubber dinghy and launching it, occupied us for another half hour. When all this was done, we took a few personal belongings and the ship's papers and climbed into the two small boats. There was still several feet of water under us as we worked our way across the reef toward the solid green jungle of the island. If we had been noticed, it wasn't evident, although during the run in we saw several canoes in the distance.

As we approached the land, I thought I could see a break in the shoreline and headed for it. We could soon see that it contained a flat piece of muddy ground on which there were several lean-to shelters. As we moved closer, it was evident there were people about. In fact, quite a number of men, women and children turned out to watch in silence as we beached the boats a few yards in front of them. The men didn't seem friendly at all and offered no help or greeting of any kind. In the background, the kids hung behind their mothers who were barebreasted and somewhat shy. There was a large open boat with an outboard tied to a stake at the water's edge.

I approached the man who seemed to be the leader of the group and in my most pleasant manner, asked him if he spoke English. He nodded, still showing no real interest in being hospitable. I said we had come from Kusaie and our boat was stranded on the reef. I pointed in the direction of where it was, which was not now visible from this indentation in the jungle. I said we needed to get to the main village of Kolonia on the other end of the island for help and that I would pay him to take us there. The offer to pay seemed to get their attention and he said he would do it and that the trip would take about an hour. With little more formality than this, we pulled our own boats up on the muddy bank, climbed into his larger boat with him and one other man and were on our way. I later learned that the man's name was Winnie Hadley and he was the son of the king of this part of the island. As we rounded the first part of the reef off his dwelling, I could see our stricken vessel lying on her side in the distance. She looked small and forlorn out there and I began to feel the first strong pangs of regret and hurt deep in my gut. I had committed a major blunder and it was to haunt me for a long time.

The trip to Kolonia seemed endless. The boat kicked up spray that kept flying over us and nothing was said for almost an hour as we threaded our way through the reefs and shallows to the north end of the island. Finally, after a final turn past a last point on the island, we headed down a narrow man-made channel toward the little town of Kolonia. There was a small derelict island schooner aground close to the town and assorted rusting iron junk along the water's edge. It was quiet this Sunday morning and not a very inviting scene as they worked the boat onto a small stretch of sand next to an old World War Two M-Boat, upturned in tall grass. Sinbad, our cat, had been terrified throughout the whole morning's experience. He had almost never been off "Evening Star" since coming aboard as a kitten and as soon as the boat ground to a halt on the sand, he bolted for the grass and ran under the rusted hulk. Although we didn't realize it at that moment, it was the last we were to see of him for a month.

A car, driven by a woman, came down the dirt road by a huge warehouse and saw us land. Curious, she came over to see who we were. When we greeted her, she agreed to help and left her passengers standing on the beach with Jeanne and Susie while she took me to seek help. Our first stop was at a house where the Ponapean Harbormaster was reclining with his wife on a porch behind mosquito netting. He suggested we go to see the "Director of Public Works" to get the needed permission for help and equipment. This took us to our next stop in the government housing section on a hill behind the town to see an American by the name of Syl Tulley. He said he could provide an LCU vessel with a powerful winch on it to help drag us off the reef if I could pay for it. I assured him I would be willing to pay whatever was necessary, and with this out of the way, we climbed into his jeep to go see the native Skipper of the LCU.

"Ramsin" was a fine looking man about thirty-five years old and a native of Mokil island. After explaining our predicament and location, he agreed to round up his crew and be at the wreck site about dark with the LCU. Syl then took me back to the waterfront to let Jeanne and Susie know what was going on. After asking the men who had brought us from the wreck to wait a while longer, we all piled into the jeep and headed for a small hotel behind the town called the "Cliff Rainbow." They gave us a room and Syl suggested we might like to have a bite to eat before I started back to the boat. At the time, it sounded like a good idea as we hadn't eaten since the night before. We went to a place called the Joy restaurant for lunch which seemed to take a long time to prepare. I was beginning to get uneasy and anxious to get back to the boat and it seemed like an eternity before we finished eating and had a lunch packed for the men waiting for me on the beach. Finally, we returned to the men on the beach and I left Jeanne and Susie to go back to the hotel and wait for my return. I had no idea how long that would be. The men ate their lunch on the move as we headed back toward Metalanim Bay where "Evening Star" lay stricken. It was now about noon.

Our first stop was at the muddy dwelling site where I picked up my two small boats noticing that one of the oars and some small hand tools were missing from them. We dropped the one man there and started for the wreck site, I following Winnie Hadley's boat in my own. As we approached, I noticed a lot of men on a piece of the reef that was dry. Apparently, there were none around "Evening Star" which was a hundred yards away, still lying in a few feet of water. Then, I spotted something else and, for the first time, realized what was happening. A mattress, my mattress, folded in half with a line tied around it, was lying on the reef close to the milling men. I had left the boat locked and in order and they had evidently broken into it and were looting.

I immediately directed Winnie Hadley to head for the mattress and retrieve it. As we got closer, I could see numerous other items of mine strewn along the dry reef. A slow rage began to build within me as I directed Winnie to retrieve my things. I tied my small boats to his, climbed onto the now dry reef and started toward the cluster of perhaps fifty men. I yelled and cursed them as I approached and they silently filed away down the reef toward their waiting canoes without replying or trying to pick up any of the things they had taken. They were mostly older men and the reason they left quietly was because their canoes were already full of my belongings. I climbed off the reef and started toward my ship as fast as I could move through several feet of water over an uneven reef. It didn't occur to me there might still be anyone aboard, but as I approached, several heads began to pop into view in the cockpit area. When I got close, I cursed them but they made no immediate move to leave. Others kept appearing until there were five young men in their early twenties either in the cockpit or standing on the ladder leading below.

At this moment, a sail sack loaded with loot was pushed through the forward hatch onto the sloping deck, followed by a sixth man. I headed for him. He turned the sack loose and it slid down to the scuppers as I grabbed the pinrail and swung up on deck. He started toward the bow but slipped and tried to jump over the side. With one hand on the pinrail and the other on the jib halyard for support, I caught him with the toe of my right foot and kicked him clean over the chain stay and into the water. I then turned my attention to the men in the aft cockpit and they were clambering over the side also by now. All except one. We both spotted the fishing spear he had left amidships by the boom gallows at the same time and started for it. He reached it first but was off balance and I got both hands on it also and wrestled him backwards over the lifeline into the water. I turned loose of the shaft as he went over in order to stay aboard and he threatened me with the spear as I fought my way toward the cockpit on the slick and sloping surface of the deck. I had cleared the deck of these fellows but I sensed their growing belligerency and for the first time, began to feel fear. It was a struggle to gain the main hatch by climbing over the now sloping mizzen mast and I made it just as a hail of coral rocks sliced toward me. Without hesitation, I dove head first through the hatchway and a huge piece of rock sliced into the hatchcombing as I went through.

I landed on a pile of debris in the chartroom. The whole area below was a shambles. In their haste to find treasure, they had emptied lockers and strewn everything throughout the whole boat. There was a mess of books, food, clothing, bedding and a hundred other items two feet deep all through the cabins. My only concern at that moment was to get to my weapons and I crawled to the forward cabin where I had a rifle stashed in a small hanging locker. The locker door was torn off and the gun was, of course, gone. There had been a small 22 calibre pistol stored under the floor boards of the locker but they were ripped out and it was gone also. My heart sank as I didn't know what might be going on outside just then. The only other weapon I had aboard was a 38 calibre pistol that always stayed under my bunk in the main cabin. I was sure that it had been taken, as the mattress was gone and the bunk area was now four feet deep in debris. I dug through it frantically anyway and to my total amazement, I felt the gun. Rage again overcame fear as I rushed topside. My fears of a few moments before were un-founded as the whole lot of them were now moving away toward the other end of the reef. They had to pass close to Winnie Hadley and my pile of retrieved gear as they went by and I fired a round in the air both out of anger and to let them know it would have been unwise for them to bother my gear. As they retreated toward their waiting canoes, I reached Winnie and sunk exhausted on the damp mattress. He just stared at me, and the gun still in my hand.

106

CHAPTER TWENTY

IT WAS TWO HOURS AFTER DARK with another high tide on the ebb and too late to try a salvage attempt even if the boat from Kolonia did arrive. I was beginning to wonder if it ever would. I huddled in the bottom of the cockpit well to stay out of the wind and seek some relief from the damp coolness of the night. Not knowing whether to expect another visit from looters, I had been there since the beginning of darkness with the gun close at hand. I had no desire to go below anyway, it was such a mess. A preliminary inspection after my ordeal in the afternoon revealed total chaos and destruction. Locker doors had been ripped off and discarded, with the contents strewn over the cabins so they could sort the things they wanted. With a boat full of people, you know there was quite a rush to get to the real treasures first and claim them. The openings to the bilges had even been thrown open and were full of debris. Many number-ten cans of dried food had been opened and the contents poured into the water in the bilges. Over this goo were all their discards: utensils, cushions from the bed and couches, tools, spare parts from the bosun's locker, and most sickening of all, hundreds of photographic slides we had been collecting for the past two years. Eight millimeter movie film which I had been collecting since my kids were toddlers was strewn the length of the boat and even in the water outside.

Before darkness fell, I had concentrated on clearing the passageways throughout the cabins and covering the bilges so you could at least walk below. I also picked up as many undamaged slides as I could dig out of the mess and put them in a paper sack. I tried to find as many of my hand tools as I could because I knew they would be of utmost importance to me in the days to come.

The sound of the surf was relentless as it crested over the sharp edge of the coral reef a couple-of-hundred-feet behind me and rolled on in small waves to slap against the bottom of the hull. At the height of the tide, a small fine spray would sometimes drift over my position in the cockpit well. I was becoming stiff from sitting so long in one spot so I crawled forward and climbed into the rigging as high as I could reach to search the blackness for some sign of a light to the north that would indicate my help was on the way. I saw nothing but darkness and heard nothing but the roar of the reef. I wondered what I would do if they failed to show up at all since I didn't dare leave the boat again. A cup of coffee would have raised my spirits but I was afraid of trying to make a fire even if I could find any coffee. The stove had been used as a stepping plat- form through the galley hatch and looked battered. It was off its gimbals and jammed into the well it usually hung in. I was sure the pipes and fittings were damaged and I had already discon- nected all gas and electricity. I was becoming too numb to feel the exhaustion that was beginning to creep over me.

The sound of a motor awakened me from a half sleep. My joints ached as I climbed out of the cockpit well to see a sixteen-foot open boat emerge from the darkness and ground on the coral twenty feet away. A man started poling his way toward the boat. His greeting was friendly and I relaxed as he threw me a line and climbed aboard. The LCU was not far behind, he said. He had come ahead in the open boat to help guide the larger one through the pass in the reef when it arrived. He took a quick turn through the crippled vessel and we both shoved off in his boat to await the arrival of the LCU. The water was already beginning to shallow as the outgoing tide drained the reef and we had some difficulty poling his boat back across it to open water where he could start the engine. By this time, the lights of the LCU appeared offshore and we headed for it. These fellows were well acquainted with these waters and they had no trouble threading the larger vessel to an anchorage inside the reef and close to the main island.

An LCU is a World War Two barge-like boat about forty feet wide and a hundred feet long with a huge ramp that opens up the whole bow for loading and unloading. The superstructure in the aft end of the boat houses the crew's living quarters, galley and engine room. Above all this is a raised deck that contains a small steel-enclosed wheelhouse and assorted winches and davits. The main piece of gear on the aft deck is a large and powerful donkey engine and winch with large spools of heavy cable. The vessel's purpose during the war was to run in as close to a beach as it could before it grounded and unload heavy equipment in shallow water. Then, the winch, which was attached to an anchor dropped in deeper water as the boat approached the beach, would literally haul the heavy barge back off into deeper water again. I hoped it would somehow do a similar service for me.

My clothes were soggy damp and I was chilled through to the bone as I stepped into the warmth of the crew's quarters about an hour before midnight. The crew consisted of seven island men, including Ramsin, whom I had met earlier. They were friendly enough but remained somewhat detached and seemed to ignore me, if anything. At this point, it just felt good to be with some friendly people and share the warmth of their galley fire. It's hard to believe that you can be so cold only six degrees above the equator but I was to find out in the days to come just how uncomfortable it can be in wet clothes on a

109

windy reef at night. The galley was located in the center of the ship and the crew's living quarters were located to either side of it. A tuna cooked whole was on the counter along with a loaf of bread, butter and jam. There was water on the stove for making instant coffee and I was told to help myself. The crew had already eaten so I fixed a plate and sat across from Ramsin at the dining table. He talked of plans for the morning and I just listened. His idea was to move the LCU back outside the reef where I had gone across it and get a large line over the reef to my boat. Then, with the aid of the big winch and a high tide, move her backward into deep water. I was too tired to find any fault with his plan at the time and he suggested I get some sleep before we had to start the operation by 0400. I didn't argue with that suggestion and climbed into an empty bunk as soon as my meal was finished. The noise of the ship and the crew joking and talking didn't keep me from falling asleep immediately.

The rest was all too brief but I felt somewhat refreshed when Ramsin awakened me at 0300. A quick cup of coffee and a piece of bread and jam was breakfast before we piled into the small boat with half the crew for the trip to my stranded boat. The tide was on it's way in and just high enough at this point to get the open boat over the reef. Since it was loaded with heavy line and assorted gear, we had to walk it across the reef sometimes in knee deep water. I couldn't help but think of the deadly poisonous Stone Fish that abide in these waters as we stumbled over the rough surface in pitch blackness. When we reached "Evening Star," the crew started poking through the litter in the cabins while Ramsin and I decided how to rig a sling off the stern to attach the heavy towing line. I wasn't too optimistic as we worked. I found out that the LCU could not be anchored outside the reef because the depths were too great so the big powerful winch could not be used for pulling me off. They would have to depend on the power of the ship's engines to drag her off. I didn't think this possible because dragging her stern first would cause the deepest part of the keel to dig into the reef's surface. If my vessel had been facing the open sea, I would have been more inclined to think it possible. As dawn broke, the water was now almost four feet deep around us and the high tide only an hour away. Ramsin was ready to go back to the LCU to get her on her way but I stopped him. As the tide rose, a small surf was building over the reef's edge and I had been watching it closely. As it broke, some of the surge of water would continue over the reef to slap against the exposed bottom of the boat while the rest would recede as backwash. Between surges, the jagged edge of the reef would be momentarily exposed and it was enough watching it to convince me that we would probably break my vessel in two as she went across that edge if indeed we were to generate enough power to move her. I had no idea of any other way to save her but I told Ramsin, no go. I would rather strip her now than take a chance of sinking her on that lip of reef. I think he agreed with me. Anyway, he didn't argue and agreed to keep the LCU there for a day to carry my gear back to Kolonia. With the vision of looters fresh in my mind, I set to work with what few tools I had to strip everything that could be taken off the boat for transport back to the waiting LCU.

It was quite a job. We completely emptied the boat below and then started on the rigging, winches, pumps and every other piece of ship's equipment that could be removed. This included the big square yardarm, the main and mizzen booms and even the galley sink. Their small open boat was loaded many times and made numerous trips back and forth across the reef to the anchored LCU. Some of the larger items like the yard and booms, we had to float away. I marveled at the energy and enthusiasm with which the men pitched in to help. They even seemed to enjoy moving and handling hundreds of items that came off the stricken vessel. Later, I was to find out why. This occupied the whole day and, during this time not a single canoe approached the scene, except one.

111

Late in the afternoon, a single canoe appeared with a good looking young man who turned out to be "Paulis," another son of the king, and brother of Winnie Hadley. Through Ramsin, I made a deal with him to stay aboard "Evening Star" and act as a guard until I returned. He agreed, and I felt much relieved to have that problem out of the way. He left to go after food and water while we continued our work. Just before dark, the job was completed and the boat was now an empty shell. The only thing left behind was two heavy batteries that there just wasn't room for on our last load. As we arrived at the LCU with this last load, Paulis rowed up in his outrigger with a sack full of supplies, ready for his first night's vigil. I didn't envy him the task but I agreed to pay him well and he was quite happy with the arrangement.

This LCU was used at Kolonia for hauling sand and there was a foot of it scattered over the main deck. In a heap on one side of the ship was all my gear laying in the sand. It made quite a pile. A rain shower was beginning to form and I immediately set to work to try to cover everything as best I could with tarps and sails. It was a sorry looking mess already and I was beginning to wonder if it was worth the effort since I had probably lost my little ship anyway. The wear of the day and physical exhaustion was again overtaking me and my final act before heading for the coffee pot and rest was to take a few pieces of personal gear like the ship's clock, barometer, compass, sextant and chronometer onto a vacant bunk where it would be safe out of the moisture. One other treasure was a small hand ax with sheath that I had found under the tool locker. The looters had missed it and somehow such an insignificant item had taken on special significance for me. I treasured it and stowed it with the other things.

Dinner was more fish and rice. Afterward, Ramsin said it was too late for the LCU to start her return trip to Kolonia and it would get an early start the following morning. He said he would take the small boat back tonight and I could accompany him or stay with the LCU. I was a little concerned about the girls and anxious for a bath and some dry clothes so I said I would go with him. It was still raining slightly as we shoved off an hour after dark for the run to Kolonia, eighteen miles away. I sat huddled in the bow of the boat for the hour-and-a-half ride and marveled at the skill of this man as he maneuvered the outboard at full speed through narrow patches of reef and shallow water in almost total darkness. Finally, after what seemed like an eternal period of time, we rounded the last point and the lights of the little town came into view. I was so cold and tired, it was with some effort that I negotiated the narrow gangplank from the boat dock to the wharf when we arrived. Ramsin drove me to the small hotel at the top of the hill and let me out. I walked toward the lighted dining room and ran into Jeanne and Susie just returning from dinner. They were surprised and delighted to see me.

They had a decent sized room and it had a bathtub. I peeled off the wet and stinking clothes I had been wearing since the night before hitting the reef and climbed into a hot tub that Jeanne had run for me. She poured me a ration of whiskey in a water glass and I savored the luxury of warmth both inside and out. They both came in and sat down, waiting and eager to know what had happened, and I told them the whole story. The final question was the hardest. "What do we do now?" With that, the final burden of what I had allowed to happen to my little family and ship engulfed me and I could hardly hold back the tears. My voice broke as I simply said, "We are badly bent at the moment but not yet broken." With that, they left me with my bath and whisky.

CHAPTER TWENTY-ONE

WITH THE MORNING CAME A NEW DAY, new energy and new hope. Even though we had arrived at the island in an unorthodox fashion, the formalities had to be observed so I presented myself at the government offices first thing and was granted pratique. Now that we were officially cleared, we needed to get word to our family and friends about what had happened. We were expecting Grant, and Dan and Ellen Blom from Seattle, to arrive by air within a few days from the mainland. They were planning to sail with us from Ponape to our next destination of New Britain and I had to get word to them before they departed. I penned a cable to Grant saying only, "Shipwrecked at Ponape. Boat probably total loss. Crew OK. Letter follows."

Jeanne left the hotel to take care of this and I headed for the docks. Without transportation, I found it to be a long walk down a hot and dusty dirt road that led from town to the end of the bay. In the days to come, I would walk that road many times in heat and rain. Nearing the docks, I passed a large open shed with a tin roof shimmering in the noon day sun. This was the airport terminal sitting at the end of an unpaved runway cut out of a coral reef. Once each week, the Air Micronesia flight from

Guam or Kwajalein landed there, the island's only real link
with the outside world. A little further along, I found the docks
and saw that the LCU had already arrived. The crew had all left
except one man. I glanced at my pile of gear lying in the sand
on deck and went into the crew's quarters to check on the items
I had stowed there. Everything seemed to be where I left them
except the hand ax. I couldn't find it and asked the crewman if
he knew where it might be. He just shrugged and I had an
uneasy feeling. At first, I had enjoyed a feeling of relief at being
in the hands of the government crew. Now, I was not so sure
that I had not been robbed again. If the hand ax was gone, how
about some of the hundreds of other items stowed on deck
under the tarps and sails? It was the first indication of what I was
faced with for the rest of my stay on Ponape.

I headed back to town to see Syl Tulley, the Director of
Public Works, who had authorized the use of the LCU a few
days before. He was again friendly and helpful and I told him of
my ordeal on the reef with looters and thieves. He readily
admitted that this was a way of life on the island and anything
that was left unattended would likely be stolen. I was dumb-
founded he didn't warn me of this at our first meeting instead
of letting me waste so much time before returning to the
unprotected vessel on the reef. I also brought up the matter of
possible theft by the LCU crew and he said he would have to
have some proof, of course, before he could take any action. He
strongly suggested I remove my gear from the LCU as quickly
as possible. How I was going to save my boat was one problem
I had no idea how to solve at the moment. Now I realized I had
another serious problem. He did give me one very welcome
piece of information. There was one man on the island who
might help me if I could persuade him to do so. He added, "He
is sometimes a difficult individual to deal with."

The man's name was Jack Adams and I made inquiries as to
where to find him. It turned out he was running a crane at the
airport so I headed back that way. I found a big raw-boned

specimen full of sweat in the cab of a crane near the docks. Everybody on the island knew by now of the predicament of the American who had wrecked his boat, and of course, this man was no exception. I stood close by his work trying to get his attention and finally he climbed down from the crane. It was a difficult place to talk because of the noise and activity but I said I needed assistance to try to salvage my vessel and was told he was the one man who might help. His reaction was to say that he was really too busy to get involved and that it was probably a hopeless project anyway. Not too many boats come off the reefs intact. We talked for awhile and he seemed to become more interested. He asked if we had a place to stay and I told him we were at the hotel but I needed a place to stow my gear from the ship. He suddenly said to meet him in about an hour when he finished his project and he would see what he could do to help. From that moment on, I knew I had a potentially valuable ally if I could get him involved.

A couple of hours later, we were in his truck heading for town to see his wife who owned a small house across the road from his warehouse and workshops. She agreed to rent the house to us and Jeanne and Susie were ecstatic to have a real home to live in after two years at sea. The place was a neat little bungalow with two small bedrooms, a kitchen and bath and large screened in porch that ran the breadth of the back of the house. We couldn't believe our good fortune. We not only had a place to sleep but also a place to stow the ship's gear. Jack had not given any indication that he would help salvage the boat but he was certainly our savior with this immediate problem. He took me in his truck to the docks and we off-loaded all my belongings from the LCU. It filled his large truck. When we finished stacking all the heavy spars, sails, anchors, chain, line and assorted gear around the perimeter of the house, it looked like a trader's store. One whole end of the inside porch was also piled high with ship's gear. That first evening, over a drink with Jack, we started to become acquainted and discuss the main problem of getting the boat off, if indeed it was possible to do so. Jack's belief was that it was possible to salvage anything with the right equipment but therein lay the problem. We were in a remote outpost of the world with limited options. I went to bed that evening feeling I had made a friend and maybe there was hope.

Jack Adams was a unique individual. I believe he found his way to this island as a young man and had married the daughter of a Belgian trader. He was a big man about sixty years old and strong as an ox. Over the next few weeks, I was to learn that his strength was not only physical, his influence on me was profound. He could be a difficult man and not much liked by some of the authorities on the island but when there was a seemingly insurmountable problem to be tackled, he was the one they turned to. He was smart and had worked with heavy equipment all his life. His warehouse was piled high with every manner of heavy equipment such as jacks, cables, heavy shackles and all the tools of his trade. He nearly always worked alone and had a habit of never asking for help on any project. He would just tackle it like he was the only human being on earth and had to figure a way to handle it alone. I have never in my life known such a self-reliant man and, to this day, I have tried to emulate him in that respect. Being liked didn't mean much to him but it was apparent that he had the respect of the islanders.

The following morning, I walked across the road to Jack's warehouse where he was busy with some project and he didn't have much to say. As was his way, he didn't ask for help on whatever he was doing but I pitched in to help in any way I could without asking. This was to be our relationship for the whole time I spent on Ponape. I was there every morning to lend a hand with whatever project he was working on. We delivered sand around the island in his dump truck, hauled diesel fuel, fixed an oil spill in the town's huge storage tank and many other things I've since forgotten. I think he came to depend on me as a capable helper and a good worker and there was mutual respect. In return, he joined us almost every evening after work over a drink to tell stories and talk about how to salvage "Evening Star." Three days after I met him, he and I, along with Ramsin, took a small boat down to the wreck to look her over and check on Paulis, my guard on the boat. A week after that, we had formulated our first plan to move her.

Ponape is a large, mountainous, verdant-green island in the eastern end of the Caroline chain. It sits about eight degrees north of the equator and is influenced only minimally by the northeast tradewind. There was a high percentage of rainfall and it was hot, humid and uncomfortable most of the time. The only town was Kolonia. Dirt roads and ramshackle buildings gave the town the look of a nineteenth-century Dodge City with palm and banana trees. The politics and administration of the islands had been dominated by foreigners for many years; first by the Germans before the First World War and then by the Japanese after 1918 when the islands were mandated to them. Currently it was administered by the United States as a Trust Territory. Almost all the improvements in roads, bridges, sewer and water systems had been built by the Japanese, and they were still in place and in use. Also, throughout the town, were the openings of numerous caves that had been built during World War Two. We could look across the road from our house and see the remains of small Japanese tanks rusting in the tall grass. With two to four-hundred inches of rainfall a year, you were subject to frequent rain showers that left everything a muddy mess. There were relatively few miles of roads and because they were so rough, it was slow going to traverse them a lot of the time. The scenery, however, was spectacular with so much greenery and flowers and always the spectacle of swollen streams rushing through the dense growth. The wild grasses that were everywhere grew at such a rapid rate, they would cover anything within a few weeks. One day, while working with Jack at the end of his warehouse, he suggested I should have some transportation to get around in and said I could have the jeep over by the corner of his building. I had not noticed any vehicle around there other than his truck, so I was totally surprised when he walked over, pushed some grass aside and revealed an old jeep with grass growing through the floor-boards. I had been only a few feet away from it for several weeks without knowing it was there.

That evening, I walked in and Jeanne handed me a cable that lifted my spirits:

"Crushed to get Jeanne's tragic letter. Keep the flag flying. Will take our Safari later. Contact Bank of Hawaii, Ponape as I cable bucks to help tide you over." —Grant

Ramsin and Jack Adams en route to my stranded vessel

CHAPTER TWENTY-TWO

WE MADE OUR FIRST ATTEMPT to move "Evening Star" only a week after I met Jack. Some of the highest tides of the year were occurring during this month so we planned to try to kedge her off the reef with anchors in the traditional manner. Of the two high tides a day, the evening one was the highest so we had to work at night. Jack concurred with me that we should try to move her in toward the island to quiet water instead of trying to take her off the edge of the reef into the open sea. That meant moving the twenty-five ton ship across nine hundred feet of hard dead reef. Even then, we would only reach a deep water lagoon that was itself completely enclosed by reef. If we could reach this lagoon and refloat her there, we had another fifty feet of reef to cross before reaching the deep water passage next to the island that had open access to the sea. We decided to take one step at a time and try to get across that nine hundred feet first. During low tide, there were only a few inches of water over the reef or it was totally dry and we could walk around the boat lying on the hard surface. With about four feet of water at high tide, it would not be possible to float the boat but we hoped we could put it on rollers and move her off on her bilges which would have some floatation. With that in mind, we used hydraulic jacks to raise her bilge a few inches and place heavy pipe casings under her.

We decided that we could only move her a short distance at a time because of a limited amount of time of high water and the need to reset the rollers every time she moved. With that in mind, we cleared a path about ten yards wide down the reef in the direction we wanted to go. It was hard work and had to be done by hand and pick to level the rough spots on the reef for our runway. My hands were raw from carrying coral rock to the side of the runway and the pile of rock on either side made a wall of coral a couple of feet high the length of our effort. We then placed our anchors well ahead of the boat and waited for high tide.

As the water rose late that night, we kept taking all the strain on our anchor lines and chain that we could, using the heavy anchor windlass on the bow and block and tackles to get a better purchase on the lines. At the height of the tide, she seemed to want to move but was only straining at the leash. Jack jumped into our open boat which had a powerful outboard engine and threw me a line which I made fast. With his engine at full power and me straining at the anchor windlass, she shuddered and lurched forward on her rollers a few feet. It was a small victory. We readjusted the strain on our tackles and repeated the process a few times. The only problem was that she moved not in the direction of our runway but angled instead toward the coral rock wall on the side of the runway. A quick inspection showed that our pipe rollers were bent and mangled and that we might have done some damage to the hull. With that discovery, we knew we had to go back to the drawing board. It was still a long way down that reef to freedom.

Another week was spent catching up with Jack's work and over whiskey in the evenings, we devised our second plan. We knew we needed more power to move the boat and decided a government M-Boat that was available might do the job. The M-Boat was a much smaller version of the LCU but without a stern winch for power. It drew less water than the LCU and we might be able to get it over the second reef into the lagoon during high tide and use her engines for pulling power. We also decided to attach watertight fifty-five gallon drums to the hull below the water line to help lift the nine-thousand pound keel off the reef. Jack arranged for me to borrow two forty-foot telephone poles from the Public Works Department. We would strap the poles to the keel and use them to hold the drums. The department was reluctant to let us have the poles and said if they were lost, I would be billed $400.00 for them. We also rounded up as many steel drums as we could find and made them watertight.

On April 28th, we loaded all our gear and supplies into the M-Boat and it left with it's own crew for Metalanim Bay. We followed in a smaller boat a couple of hours later and arrived late in the afternoon to meet them. After much maneuvering, it was apparent we were not going to be successful in getting the M-Boat across the reef, even at high tide. Since our whole plan depended on that being accomplished, we couldn't do any-thing but send the vessel back to Kolonia. The rest of the afternoon and far into the evening, we worked to clear more of our runway. About two in the morning, after lashing the heavy poles to my stricken vessel for safekeeping, we headed for home ourselves.

I awoke Jeanne at four o'clock in the morning and had her fix our breakfast. Jack and I then slept for an hour before heading back to Metalanim Bay. We were working against the tides and that didn't allow us much time for rest. The tide was low and the vessel high and dry when we arrived and the telephone poles had disappeared. I could not believe they had been washed away and we searched the shoreline of the nearby island to no avail. Two forty-foot telephone poles don't just disappear so I concluded they had been taken. Paulis had been sent home the night before for a break from his guard duties and obviously, that was a mistake. Paulis was now back to help and we rigged our jacks again and removed the mangled pipes from under the boat. It was obvious the hull had been damaged under the port side and the vessel was taking water during the high tides. So much so that she never rose off the reef with the tides any longer. The engine and everything on that side of her were now partly immersed in sea water half of every day she lay there wounded. The water was now rising again on a flood tide so we had to wait for evening to tackle the hull problem. In the meantime, we rigged a portable generator on the rocks next to the boat and continued working on our runway. Low tide occurred about ten that evening and we fired up the generator for lights and went to work. I will always remember lying under that giant hull in six or eight inches of water to tack a thin piece of plywood with small nails and quick drying cement to the leaking hull. There was hardly room to swing a hammer and work, and I hoped one of those jacks wouldn't give way and crush an arm or a head. When the job was done, Jack and I headed back to Kolonia in the middle of the night for more telephone poles. We drove his forklift through the sleeping town to the big Public Works storage yard and helped ourselves to two more specimens. I kept looking over my shoulder to see if someone was going to storm in and stop us. It didn't happen and we took the poles to the dock, rolled them into the bay and tied them together for towing by our small boat. It was a long slow trip back to the reef with the heavy poles and we made it a little before daylight.

All the next day was spent working the heavy poles under the turn of the bilges, one on either side. They were attached to the keel by suspending them on heavy cables from the deck above. This gave us something to lash our watertight barrels to and we hung as many as we could around the boat and as tight to the keel as possible. When the tide came in again, our patch on the hull held and the boat again rose with the water. We found the watertight barrels would not lift the keel although it did take some of the weight off and we hoped it would lighten her enough to help. The following high tide would be greater but would not occur until four o'clock the next morning so again we waited and worked on the runway. In the wee hours of the morning, our tide reached it's highest and with it came a fifteen knot wind and some wave action which might help. We tried the same procedure with anchors and power from the small boat and after much straining, moved her another twenty feet. The result was the same; she moved off our runway and again rested against the rock piles on the side but with no damage to the hull this time.

At daylight, we were exhausted and headed back to Kolonia for some much needed rest. As we left "Evening Star," she looked terrible with those telephone poles lashed to her bilges and drums hanging all over her. I was despondent. In two weeks, we had moved her only about forty feet but still had over eight hundred feet to go and then, uncertainty. I needed a drink badly and cursed myself for not having the foresight to bring along some spirits.

CHAPTER TWENTY-THREE

THIS WAS NOW OUR THIRD WEEK on Ponape and with two unsuccessful attempts to salvage the boat, I needed a chance to rest and recuperate from the rigors of the past ten days. Jeanne and I both rode the truck and hauled sand for Jack and I continued to help him all I could on whatever project he was working on. We also had some time to ourselves.

Jeanne had settled into the life of the little town and made some friends. Russ and Rene Varner had a house across the road from us and were nice neighbors. Rene was the sister of Jack Adam's wife, Evette. It was a small tightly-knit community with only a handful of Americans working for the Trust Territory Government. They included us in all their social gatherings while we were there; a party at the Varners and a barbecue at the Syl Tulley's. At these gatherings, we met the whole American community which included the local judge and some of his staff as well as other administrative people. There was very little said to me about our predicament at these gatherings. It was somewhat of a political thing with the Ponapean officials because of the looting and thefts, and I understood. Being preoccupied with the problems I was facing, I don't think I was very good company during this time but

Jeanne was the moderating influence and was well-liked. They enjoyed her company even if they had to put up with the unsociable deadhead she was with.

Jeanne and I had a day together with no work for a change and went to the "Joy" restaurant for lunch. Afterward, we walked to the airport to watch the weekly plane arrive which was a big event. There was always a crowd of islanders to meet the plane which was usually full of officials from one island or another. It was on this day that we first met Bob and Patti Arthur. They had been cruising sailors like ourselves at one time and had settled on Ponape to build a hotel using only islanders to help them. Their hotel was about five miles from Kolonia on a beautiful bluff overlooking the offshore reefs. It was called the "Village" and that's what it looked like. The complex consisted of individual cottages made from local materials and constructed using Ponapean building techniques. There was a large thatched dining room and bar that was magnificent as a place to spend the evening. Their "Village" was still under construction when we were there and I wondered who in the world would ever find their way to this out-of-the-way place looking for a hotel. They had their dream though and I, of all people, understood dreams. They had a daughter, Janet, whom Susie had already met and visited with. When the Arthurs picked up some arrivals off the plane and loaded them into the back of a pickup truck for the trip to their place, we were given a lift home since the one main road went by our house. Bob and Patti were to become very good friends and I owe them a great debt of gratitude for the help, both materially and spiritually, they gave us through our ordeal on Ponape.

A few days of rest helped my mental attitude and on May 4th, I was ready to take another look at the ship. My spirits were further lifted that morning when Ramsin came by and returned some of the items taken by members of his crew. It wasn't much; a compass and a power saw, but it was a start and I appreciated his help. We had tried to take an inventory of things removed from the boat and although it wasn't complete, we found many items missing.

Jeanne had not been back to the stricken vessel since our disaster on the reef and insisted on going with Jack and I to see what was going on. We headed for the Arthur's first. Bob loaned us one of his boats and I hired a nice young Ponapean by the name of "Alex" to go with us and lend a hand. Leaving from their place cut a lot of distance off the run to Metalanim Bay. It was a hot day and when we reached "Evening Star," you could smell the stench that came from within her hull. I think it was a shock for Jeanne to see the home she had so lovingly kept in beautiful shape for so long. Down below, the bilges were full of rotting dried food and covered with bugs and flies. The smell was not pleasant. Being Jeanne, she immediately started the cleanup and I marvelled at this girl from a genteel background down on her knees dipping that awful goo out of the bilges with her bare hands. While she worked below, the men and I worked to clear rocks and debris from under the boat and prepare her for another salvage attempt. Jack and I had sat long into the previous night and talked of another plan to move her. We were all very tired, hot and dirty when we finally arrived late that evening at our house in Kolonia to find that Susie had a good curry dinner waiting for us.

CHAPTER TWENTY-FOUR

J ACK AND I NOW HAD A PLAN that we thought might work. We needed time to prepare for it and the following week was spent working with him and preparing for what I figured would be a final effort. The full moon and the final spring high tide of the season was due on May 14th and that was our target date. Without any high water over the reef to work with and the Western Hurricane season fast approaching, we would either get her off or abandon the effort if we failed. She would then become another victim, like so many I had seen on reefs all over the Pacific. Although I never mentioned it to anyone, I intended to burn her where she lay if that happened rather than let the scavengers have her beautiful mahogany and oak timbers. It would be my final act of defiance.

We abandoned the idea of using telephone poles under the bilges because they had proved to be too heavy and tended to grind into the coral reef hampering our efforts rather than helping. We towed them back to Bob Arthur's on our last return trip and now Susie and I went down one day and, with Alex's help, towed them back to Kolonia. I was already committed to pay $400.00 for the first two we had lost so I was glad to get these back to the Department of Public Works. Our new plan was to cut some heavy wire cables to the proper length and secure them all the way around the boat just above the bottom of the keel. We would also use these cables to secure our watertight drums. We needed more drums and I scoured the island looking for discarded ones. They had to be made watertight and have an eye welded on them so there was a way to attach the cables. It was an exhausting week and I felt the pressure of this final effort approaching. The weather was hot and humid and we worked very long-hard days. An excerpt from my journal of May 8th:

"Worked with Jack Adams all day. Started with an oil spill from a huge storage tank in the morning that had us both full of oil and grime and ended with us trying to fix two flat tires on his forklift until eight this evening. Jeanne holding dinner."

Our new plan involved using the LCU again. We needed the power of that winch on her stern. This time, we would use a bulldozer to break into the reef that would let us into the enclosed lagoon. It would be a tricky and dangerous job to cut a path through that reef wide enough to get the LCU through but Jack thought it could be done if we got the right man on the bulldozer. He had the man. Once into the lagoon with the big LCU, we would anchor her and get cables the eight hundred feet or so to my boat. I had no trouble arranging for the LCU and bulldozer. This was all extra money for the crews and equipment and they welcomed it. There was one other problem. I needed permission from the Trust Territories High Command to cut into that reef with the bulldozer. I wired their headquarters on Siapan, asking for the needed permission and suggesting that since the reef was a dead one, it would allow the local fishermen access to the lagoon by boat for the first time. We received the following reply:

"ITEPB concurs with required dredging to save vessel 'Evening Star' aground at Metalanim Bay. Permission granted on emergency basis to proceed with salvage operation ASAP. Upon completion of salvage and dredging suggest channel be properly identified and marked and be maintained for year-around small craft use."

Everything was going too smoothly and we scheduled the LCU to depart for the wreck on May 11th. At the last minute, with all our gear aboard, we hit a big snag. Our bulldozer operator would not be allowed to drive the machine. It had to be done by the government men. The bulldozer was sitting on the beach in front of the open ramp of the LCU and the regular operator and his supervisor would not budge on their position. I pleaded with them to relent but they would not. Jack had told me this was the key to our plan and required a skillful man with a little courage. Our man fit the bill perfectly so I left everyone standing around and headed to Syl Tulley's office. He stood firm for awhile until I convinced him it was useless to even waste our efforts and money without him giving in on this stand. He knew it would create some trouble for him with his men but he wrote me an order for the supervisor. I breathed a sigh of relief and rushed back to the waiting LCU and crew. We drove the bulldozer up into the LCU and they raised the ramp and put to sea. I headed back to Jack's workshop and we worked until late that night with some final welding and preparation.

The next morning, it was blustery with a weather change in the offing. It was the beginning of the hurricane season and there was a tropical depression gathering to the north of the island. This is the area just north of the equator where a lot of these storms form before moving westerly. I hoped this one would not interfere. We were not quite finished with our welding job and worked until noon to complete it. Then, we climbed into the small boats and were on our way. I said good-

130

bye to Jeanne. She wished us luck and I felt sorry for her having to wait and wonder at the outcome. We both knew it was our last chance to save our vessel.

Upon arrival late in the afternoon, Jack took charge of the operation and had Ramsin drive the LCU right up to the edge of the reef. With full power to keep her on the edge, they lowered the giant ramp and drove the heavy bulldozer onto the reef. I went out to "Evening Star" to get her ready, make final preparations and await the outcome of the dredging operation. It did take some doing to scoop out a channel about fifty feet wide with the bulldozer and a bit of courage to open that last scoop on both sides of the reef that let the water in. A miscalculation there would have sent both the machine and the driver into deep water. We were lucky to have the right man for the job. It was completed before dark and in the last light, Ramsin drove his vessel through and anchored her firmly on the other side of the lagoon just short of our reef. So far, so good.

Bob Arthur arrived unsolicited with thirty young Ponapean men before dark to help and we laid heavy cable and line the eight hundred feet to the boat. We worked half the night in a cold rain to get everything ready and when Jack was satisfied we had everything in place, he went back to the LCU to take charge of the winching operation. We had men strung out along the length of the cable to watch for snags and pass information between me and the LCU. Finally, it was high tide and raining slightly. I crouched in the bow of the boat sopping wet and watched that cable come to life and slowly take up the slack. With the rain showers, we didn't have a moon and it was hard to see past the first man along our line back to the LCU. I could feel Jack taking up the slack slowly. He knew he could tear the bow out of the boat if it were done too suddenly. The tension increased until the cable and line were as stiff as solid rod but we didn't move. Jack sent word that he would have to give it a strong tug if we were to get it started moving and for me to stand clear should something give way. I backed off, braced myself by the mainmast and waited. The cable sprang to life with a whine and the boat lurched a few feet ahead. Then another lurch and we were moving slowly with the drums scraping and banging along the hard coral surface. Although no one could hear me, I was yelling at the top of my lungs, "Don't stop, keep her moving." By dawn, after several similar efforts, we had moved her half the distance to the lagoon. She was moving down our runway but edging into the coral rocks along the sides. At this point, we stopped to rest and reposition the LCU. We also had to wait for another high tide before continuing. I felt we had a good chance for success now, with the only other major obstacle that of being able to take her off the edge of the reef into the deep water of the lagoon. Again, I silently thanked the man who built this vessel with all her strength. I felt she wanted to see deep water again and I owed her that chance.

I didn't get to bed until almost sunup, dead tired but excited and elated about the previous night's work. At mid-morning, I awoke to find Ramsin and crew already repositioning and re-anchoring the LCU. We had to move her a little farther away from the reef and positioned her to get a better angle of pull so as to keep "Evening Star" moving in the direction we wanted her to move on the runway. Afterwards, there was not much to do but wait for the next high tide which was due to occur several hours before dawn the following morning. I was anxious to see what damage had been done to the boat in moving her so far and went out to take a look. The drums hanging all over her were dented and some smashed up pretty badly but we hadn't lost any. The only damage to the boat seemed to be some awful looking scars in her hull caused by the chaffing from the drums. I inspected her carefully and she was still watertight. Our temporary repair to the hull was holding. We spent the afternoon refastening some of the drums and further clearing any rough spots on our runway. With an evening meal out of the way, we dozed, watched the tide climbing higher over the reef and waited.

About 0130 in the morning of our second day, with everything in place and I again in the bows of the boat, the tension on
the cable pulled taut, started her moving again and she never
stopped. I held my breath as she approached the lip of the
lagoon reef, nosed over it and with a loud crash of drums
banging on the lip of coral, came upright for the first time in a
month and settled in the deep water of the lagoon. I dived
below decks to see if we were taking water but found no
evidence of it. A native diver was already checking the hull
outside and we were all cheering our success. With "Evening
Star" now under tow by a small boat, the LCU hauled her
anchors and proceeded across the lagoon, through the man
made channel over the reef and re-anchored on the other side.
The only obstacle remaining was our newly made channel
through this final piece of reef. It was about seventy feet across
and there was not quite enough water to float us. With the pull
from the LCU"s winch, we dragged her into the channel on the
last of the tide. In a few minutes, she was across and lurched
over the other lip of coral to settle upright again in deep water.
This was the channel close to the island that led through the
pass to the open sea. We had done it. We were finally free.

The heavy cables around her keel were cut away and the
drums and lines removed. She sat there like a big indignant
walrus that had just emerged from battle. Her hull and topsides
were gouged and scratched, her bilges stunk from within but
she was victorious and back in her element. I took a silent vow
never to treat her so shabbily again. It was just after first light
and before sunrise when we headed out the pass, under tow by
the LCU, and started our run up the island to Kolonia. I took a
last look at the reef and could see the long lines of coral rock
that defined our runway just emerging above the receding tide.
It is still there today.

Jack Adams owned an old rusty steel barge tied up close to
the main shipping dock and we tied "Evening Star" alongside
it. It was raining again now and there was nobody around to

greet our arrival for which I was thankful. I just wanted to be alone with my little ship for awhile. Jack picked me up in his truck a while later and we worked in heavy rain all afternoon off-loading our gear and equipment from the LCU, just the two of us, sopping wet and straining to carry the heavy cable and equipment to his truck. I thanked my lucky stars that I had met such an unselfish and capable man in my hour of need. He acted like it was just another day's work but I knew he was as elated and proud of the accomplishment as I was. He had never asked or even mentioned payment of any kind for his help. In my mind, there was no way to really repay him. When we were finished, he said we could unload the truck in the morning and he dropped me off back at the boat. I worked around her until dark to get some things squared away, then walked the whole way home in heavy rain. Without transportation, Jeanne had been unable to get to the boat because of the weather. I arrived to find Ramsin and his wife visiting with Jeanne and waiting for me. I wrote checks for him and his crew, tried to eat a little dinner and fell into bed exhausted but happy.

PART FOUR
Deliverance

CHAPTER TWENTY-FIVE

WITH THE BOAT OFF THE REEF and afloat again, I had only one goal in mind. That was to leave Ponape and get her back to Seattle. This would be no small task as the boat was crippled and unable to put to sea. I had no immediate idea what the extent of the damages were but I did know that a lot of needed supplies and equipment had been stolen. I also knew it was a major voyage of some six thousand miles home. It was to be another month of hard work before we finally departed but the next morning, we began the first steps to put our vessel and our lives back together.

I awoke with a start. In my exhaustion of the night before, I had left the boat with several hundred feet of heavy anchor chain exposed on deck. It was vital equipment and I cursed myself for letting my guard down and vowed not to let it happen again before we cleared this place. I jumped into my clothes and with a thermos of coffee, headed down the road through town and to the docks. To my great relief, the chain had been undisturbed. Maybe it was too heavy to be taken easily. Jeanne showed up later in the morning with Paulis in tow and the three of us worked all day cleaning up below decks. It was an awful, sickening job. The bilges still contained a lot of rotten food and debris and there were thousands of dead flies and bugs intermixed with the evil smelling goo. A lot of it extended into inaccessible places throughout the boat and even after the matter was removed and the wood cleaned, the stench remained. It was to take many more scrubbings with disinfectant before the cabins were livable and, to this day, if I stick my head deep enough under the cabin sole, I can still get a faint whiff of that awful time. It was a productive day and a good start when we finally headed home before dark for a drink and dinner. Nothing could dampen our enthusiasm at the moment and our good fortune in having the boat back. It was such an important part of our whole being. We had not even dared to think what life would be like starting over without her.

The next several days were spent cleaning up the boat and getting my energy back. The last few days on the reef had taken a toll. I was healthy and strong but routine life for us on Ponape was not easy without transportation. It was about two miles from the house to the boat and I walked it frequently. It was not an uncommon sight in the next few weeks to see me on the dirt road that led first to town and then down the long stretch to the docks, loaded with everything I could carry. It was either very hot from the sun and humidity or a wet walk through the frequent rain showers. My memory of these days is one of constant sweat or sopping wet. Jeanne and Susie helped on the cleanup but most of the work for the next couple of weeks fell to me. I had to methodically put the ship back in working order. All hardware and gear reinstalled, pumps repaired, running rigging put back in place, anchors and chain restowed, the galley put back in some degree of working order and a hundred other jobs. Some of them were major problems.

I cleaned the engine and engine room as best I could but there was a lot of rust and corrosion from the immersion in salt water on the reef. I had only one heavy battery for starting power and it had to be coaxed back to life. After many hours of charging with my portable generator which had miraculously survived the thieves, I was able to get the engine started. Large amounts of black smoke emerged from the exhaust but it ran. The galley was another problem. Our stove was totally destroyed and I hung an old piece of plywood in the stove well on two sticks so that it would swing like gimbles. I installed a small one-burner primus stove. Pieces of equipment like this and the portable generator had survived only because they had been stowed in the lazarette under the cockpit. The only access to that large stowage place was through a hatch behind the ladder and the thieves had not discovered it.

The other major problem was the hull itself. I dove under the boat in clear water and surveyed the damage. It was not a pretty sight. The deadwood around the keel was torn and mangled pretty badly in some places and the underside of the hull had large areas of wood planking scraped partway through from the chaffing of the heavy drums. Our temporary patch was

Surveying hull damage under water

holding but being only thin plywood, it would have to be replaced before the boat could put to sea. I called on Ramsin to come down and take a look at the problem. As a Mokil islander, he came from some of the best boat builders in the Pacific and I trusted his judgement. Even though the deadwood in the keel looked bad, he didn't think it would be a problem as far as affecting seaworthiness but the temporary patch had to be removed and the hull replanked in that area. There was no way to haul the boat. We could only careen her on a sand beach at low tide and we considered that. Then, I had an idea which I presented to him. If I could lay the boat far enough over on her side to expose the work area, could we work at the waterline to do the necessary replanking? He said it could be possible so I rigged a double block and tackle from the top of the mainmast and carried the bitter end of it away to the farther end of the barge we were tied to. With the help of several men on that line, we pulled "Evening Star" over in a heeling position as far as our strength would move her. An inspection revealed we had the temporary patched area exposed with a few inches to spare. Ramsin's father in law, Moses, worked at the government carpenter shop and agreed to help us on the weekend.

At this point, another stroke of luck came my way. A man by the name of Howard Ebert who was a teacher at the local school came by and hailed me from the barge. He said he had some heavy pieces of mahogany wood at his shop and also a gallon of unopened dolphanite bedding compound. These were treasures beyond compare to me then and I lost no time in getting over to the shop to claim them. He said he was heading home to the states in a few days and that the Ponapean students would open a can of something like the bedding compound and use it one time, leaving the lid off or loose and ruining the rest. All these things were furnished by the U. S. Government for free and they had no respect for their value. He felt I would make better use of it and I thanked him profusely. On the following Saturday, Ramsin and Moses came down and we hauled the boat over with our tackle. Then, working from my rubber dinghy tied tightly alongside, we removed the temporary patch, so difficult to put in place on the reef, and replanked the open area with inch-and-a-quarter mahogany strips. There was no power and everything had to be done with hand tools in the old manner. These men skillfully shaped three planks and they fit like a glove. Using bedding compound and heavy screws for fastenings, the job was completed in a day.

That evening, we had a surprise. After a late dinner, we were preparing to go to bed when there was a knock on the door. Jeanne answered it. A rain shower had just passed over and there stood a young Micronesian man, dripping wet with a black animal in his arms. The thing was in a pitiful state, emaciated, dirty, sopping wet and without much life in him. The man asked Jeanne if it was her cat. She did not recognize it and said she thought not. I was looking over her shoulder and said, "I think it's Sinbad. Take him." The man handed over our long lost cat and departed. We were overjoyed to have him back and glad to know he had not met some awful fate. Within a few days, with a little food and some TLC, he was romping around like always as if nothing had happened and doing his part in rat control.

By June 5th, after three weeks of hard work, the boat was ready for us to move back aboard. I was tired from all the effort and worried about what our next move should be. I knew we needed some extensive repairs to the hull and the previous week I had wired the authorities at Kwajalein in the Marshall Islands for permission to enter the island for repairs. It was the only major U. S. Government Navy facility in this part of the world and our only hope for needed help. So far I hadn't received a reply. Dave Lowe, the Public Defender for the Trust Territory on Ponape offered to help me prepare a case against the local authorities in hopes it would prompt some recovery or restitution for the hundreds of items stolen from us. He wrote the following letter on our behalf:

June 8, 1976
To whom it may concern
Re: W. A. Corley and Sailing Vessel, Evening Star.

This office represents W. A. Corley, a U. S. citizen who is the owner and skipper of the 48-foot ketch Evening Star, currently moored in the harbor at Ponape, E.C.I. Our representation concerns incidents which occurred in this district after the Evening Star went aground on the reef in Ponape in April, 1976.

The Corley family and their boat was ruthlessly victimized through theft and vandalism. They were even more ruthlessly victimized by gross nonfeasance by numerous officers and officials of the Trust Territory government. These actions have resulted in damages in the thousands of dollars and certain irreparable harm to the family and their boat. This office is preparing to file all necessary legal actions against all parties concerned, including the Trust Territory. However, this process requires substantial pre-complaint investigation. Also, as soon as the complaint is ready to file, the responsible parties will be given an opportunity to rectify, to the extent possible the harm done. This office will not tolerate any illegal or unlawful intimidation or harassment to the Corley family. We can and will take any legal step necessary to prevent and correct such an occurrence. We are prepared to act reasonably with those who wish to do likewise but will use the full power of the courts to prevent any further injustice. Should any further information be desired on this matter, please contact the undersigned directly.

David W. Lowe—Assistant Public Defender

This was a strong letter and I appreciated it but I had appealed to the local authorities and they had ignored me completely. We had reliable witnesses and knew who the culprits were but it seemed not to matter. I thought it was a waste of time to pursue it further. Dave said I should not pay any more bills due to individuals or to the government until there was some action on our case. I suggested I put up a bond in the amounts owed to show good faith but he said it wasn't necessary.

With the help of Jack's truck we moved the last of the heavy gear from the house, along with our personal belongings, to the boat. The first day, it was all we could do to just get aboard, there was so much gear piled high on the decks and on the barge. The next day, we started stowing everything. An excerpt from my journal of that day tells our mood:

"A miserable day with steady rain and black skies. Trying to get all the gear we brought aboard yesterday stowed and out of the weather. Very slow going. Susie pretty sick with a sore throat and Jeanne very despondent. I don't think she is going to stand up to this very much longer. I probably should put her and Susie on a plane and send them home. I think I can go it alone."

The following morning I said what was on my mind and Jeanne reluctantly agreed when I promised to find crew before departing. She headed for town to give the house we just left a final cleaning and to stop by the airport to check on Thursday's flight. I worked all day on rigging the boat for sail. Susie was still sick, nursing a very bad sore throat. When Jeanne returned that afternoon, she told me there was no space on a plane for another three weeks. I didn't know how long it would take to get the boat repaired at Kwajalein or if we even could. After that, it was a long month or more sail back to the U. S. mainland. I couldn't chance waiting any longer and getting caught in the first winter weather in the North Pacific as fall approached. We both went to bed that night wondering the same thing: Now what?

The next day we both felt better and so did Susie. We took it easy for a change and I went to town later in the morning to see Dave Lowe and inquire about my request to enter Kwajalein. Still no answer. I walked back to the boat in the afternoon and noticed a small ship named "Micronesian Sunrise" tied up at the main ship's dock. She was unloading fuel. Jeanne was in a good mood and said she had a surprise for me. She opened our ice box which had been without ice for some time and produced twelve bottles of cold San Miguel beer, a gift from the skipper of the ship I had just seen. We also had an invitation to dine aboard that evening. There's nothing like an evening out to lift the spirits of any woman. The skipper was a Philippino man by the name of Roman Davis and we, of course, accepted his hospitality. We had a fine dinner served in a rather humble looking ship's dining room and swapped stories. He also let me copy an up-to-date chart of Kwajalein island while we were aboard. His home was in the southern Philippines where he had a wife and family. Jeanne was surprised when he asked her if she would write to his wife. It seemed she was lonesome with him gone for long periods of time and loved to receive letters from people he met. Jeanne agreed and did pen a letter to her unknown friend the next day. There is a small Philippino community on Ponape and Roman either had a friend or relative there. After dinner, we went with him to visit them along with some of his crew and had a fine evening drinking and singing. The next morning, the dock was empty when we went on deck. His ship had departed in the wee hours of the morning. He couldn't have known what his act of friendship meant to us.

Jeanne and Susie were both feeling much better and with the prospects of leaving immanent, they had decided to stay with the ship. Jeanne had been cooking on the small one burner primus for the past week and I decided to try to better that situation for her. I found and purchased two small single burner propane stoves from the local trading store and installed them.

They sat proudly side by side on the old piece of plywood hanging in the galley and she was as happy as if I had bought her something grand. The simple things of life took on new meaning in a situation like ours. And to top it off, another night out. We accompanied Russ and Rene Varner to the Arthur's Village Hotel for a last dinner with them.

The next morning, June 11th, I figured it was now or never. I had done all I could to prepare our vessel for sea with what I had to work with. I visited Dave Lowe and advised him of our intention to leave for Kwajalein even though official permission had not been forthcoming. He said he would contact me there as things developed. Then I paid a final visit to Jack Adams to say good-bye and write him a check for a thousand dollars. There was really no way I could adequately repay him for what he had done for me. Later, at the government offices, I presented myself and requested a ship's clearance to leave. They didn't hesitate and issued the necessary papers.

We spent the afternoon taking on final provisions and making the ship ready for sea. Before we were finished, a man arrived at the boat saying he was from the Micronesian Legal Services Corporation and demanded payment of a bill of $153.92 in unpaid wages to two Micronesian men who were part of the LCU crew. I had withheld the final wages for these two because I learned it was they who had stolen some important items from me. I referred him to Dave Lowe, as my attorney, to present his demands and he left. Within the hour, we slipped our moorings and without looking back, raised sail and headed for the pass through the reef and the open sea for whatever lay ahead of us.

CHAPTER TWENTY-SIX

K WAJALEIN LAY SIX HUNDRED MILES to windward and they had a promise of being long difficult miles as we cleared the reef at the entrance to Ponape harbor and bore off close hauled northeastward. It soon became apparent we would have to rely on the engine to lay a direct course against the prevailing easterly winds. I fired up the diesel amid a lot of black smoke from the exhaust and, under reduced power, slowly made our way through the first night. As soon as we cleared the quiet water inside the lagoon and reached the open sea, we began to ship water in our bilges. I turned on the pumps at frequent intervals to control it but it was a source of concern to me. There were no real holes in our hull but the caulking in our planking had suffered in many places and we were taking water through these weak areas. Nothing significant at that moment but I watched it closely and slept very little that first night.

The morning of our second day, it was apparent we were not making much headway against the prevailing wind and current so I raised sail again and found our only course available to be northward. After a few hours under sail I noticed we were taking much more water because of the strain on the hull from the rigging and decided if we were to make Kwajalein safely, it

would have to be under power no matter how slowly our
progress. I also encountered another problem. The filters on
the bilge pumps kept filling up with debris from the many
hidden and inaccessible places within our hull and I had to
clear them frequently. After doing this many times in an effort
to keep the pumps functioning, I gave up and resorted to
bailing the water out with a bucket. This was hard work. I
would stand on deck and lower a bucket on a line to Jeanne or
Susie stationed below. They would fill the bucket from the
open bilge and I would haul it up and empty it over the side. We
found ourselves doing this at frequent intervals now to control
the constant flow from leakage through the hull. I debated if we
should turn back but we were managing all right and each hour
put us farther away from Ponape and closer to where we really
wanted to reach. We plowed on. An excerpt from my journal on
the second morning:

"Had a bad neck ache on my night watch. Probably from
hauling water out of the bilge, but I feel better this morning.
Good day with wind and seas down and even occasional flat
water. Noon position puts us only about four hundred miles
from Kwajalein."

We had settled into our work routine by now and were
getting our sea legs after many weeks ashore so we felt confi-
dent moving along at five knots in flat water and tropic sunshine. These conditions only lasted a day and the following
morning we had to throttle back on the engine as it was
belching too much black smoke and carbon. It was still a
beautiful day but the wind was back up and our progress
slowed.

My constant nagging worry was that the engine would fail
us entirely. If that happened, our alternatives would have
been few. We could either turn back downwind for Ponape or
bear off for the north Pacific and its westerly winds and the

long sail home. With the boat in an uncertain condition for the rigors of sail, I hoped I would not have to face that decision. On June 15th, four days out of Ponape, my journal again tells the story:

"Engine running steady so it looks as if we may make Kwajalein after all. I've had my doubts these past two days. Today's noon position puts us about two hundred miles away. Crew morale pretty good and I'm getting stronger by the day."

The previous night was one of increased wind and choppy seas and the last twenty four hours had netted us only about seventy miles. The wind and sea continued to rise and the following twenty four hours netted us only forty miles. With the increased motion of the boat, we were taking more water than usual so our work increased with the bailing effort and we were getting tired. I listened to the constant sound of the engine grinding away and hoped it would continue to perform. We were so close, but without it, our ability to reach the island and safety was doubtful so I continued to run it at very low power. Conditions hadn't changed by noon of the 16th but we were still plugging away and only ninety miles from our destination. I was getting close to being within radio range of the Navy facility and felt better. I tried to contact Kwajalein control but received no answer.

With the evening hours came less wind and unsettled weather. Our speed picked up and we tackled those last miles with renewed confidence. At first light, I strained to see any sight of the Atoll but could not make it out until an hour later. These atolls are so low lying, you are almost upon them before sighting the tops of coconut palms and we were approaching "Gea" pass into the atoll by 0800. I tried again to contact the island on the radio but still received no answer and suspected it was not working. We hadn't been sighted and were approaching a restricted Navy facility without authorization but that was the least of my concerns at the time.

Kwajalein is the largest atoll in the world with a lagoon some fifty miles long. It is a strategic U. S. Military base in this part of the Pacific and also our downwind missile range for the Vandenberg Missile facility in California. I had landed here many times as a young Navy radio operator, flying with the Military Air Transport Service over 25 years before. It was a horrible place to visit at that time, only a few years after the war. There was not a tree on it then, having been bombed to nothingness before the marines and army landed to almost wipe out the Japanese garrison. There had been thousands of Japanese buried on the island and the drinking water stunk. Fortunately, our stops during that time were only overnight but I didn't envy the personnel that were stationed there for a year at a time. I had no idea what the place was like now as we entered the pass in the reef and headed for the main island ten miles down the lagoon.

It began to rain as we threaded our way past the reefs and headed for the Navy port. With reduced visibility from the showers, we were not spotted or challenged until we were almost to the island. An astonished harbor pilot hailed us only a few hundred yards from the docks asking who we were and where we were from. I replied that we were seven days out of Ponape, taking water and could use some help. He said to follow him and led us to a mooring along their main dock. We were immediately boarded by the harbormaster and customs officials. After explaining our plight, they were most friendly and said we had come to the right place. "We can fix this vessel up like new for you. Welcome to the island and make yourselves at home. When you are ready, come down to the yard office and we'll talk about what to do." We were happy to suddenly be back where we could experience American goodwill. It was then that I felt our ordeal was really over and we were back in control again.

The area surrounding us was not what I remembered from the past. The main dock was a massive structure with a huge crane sitting on the end of it. A couple of seagoing tugs were directly across from us and other assorted shipping was near by. The water was as clear as a looking glass and a beautiful emerald green with white sand and coral below. The immediate area surrounding the harbor was bristling with huge dish antennas and clean impressive buildings. There were now trees and flowers along the streets and on the grounds around the structures. It could have been a harbor in Hawaii of thirty years before.

Jeanne and Susie were getting our little home in order in anticipation of going ashore to see the sights and I headed for the offices at the other end of the dock. As I arrived at the gate, the guard said there were some men who wanted to see me and a Micronesian Sheriff approached with a half dozen deputies in tow. He said I was under arrest along with the boat and to accompany him back to the boat. He would take us to "Ebye" island to be charged. I was stunned when he handed me the court order saying I was to be held because of the $163.00 bill owed on Ponape. I told him that there must be some mistake. I was represented by counsel on Ponape and he should be contacted immediately. The sheriff just kept repeating, "you are under arrest. Now let's go back to your boat." I asked the guard nearby where the commanding officer's office was and he pointed down one of the streets leading from the harbor. I told the Sheriff I wanted to see the commanding officer of the base before I left the island with him but he said, "No. You are under arrest and must come with me." I yelled at an astonished Jeanne who was close by that I was being arrested and that I was going to see the base commander and to stay with the boat. I then ignored the sheriff and started up the road. He and his men stayed right with me but made no effort to restrain my movements. He just kept repeating his favorite saying. As the whole entourage passed the harbor office, I could see them standing at the window wondering what this was all about and what kind of criminal they had just welcomed so generously. I was embarrassed but stalked on at a brisk stride. When I walked into the CO's office, I told the outer office clerk that I was an American citizen seeking the protection of the U. S. Government and wanted to see the head man. I was still in my sea clothes, having not had a chance to change or bathe and must have seemed somewhat of a shoddy looking character entering his office escorted by a bevy of Micronesian sheriffs.

He listened to my complaint and said he couldn't do anything for me at the moment. I would have to accompany these men to their island of "Ebye" until the thing was worked out. I simply said, "No. I seek the protection of my government and will not be taken from this island without it's being done by force. It will become a nasty mess for you and, I suspect, dire consequences if you allow me to be taken." We were at an impasse and the argument went on. I requested he allow someone to go to my boat and bring my papers from Ponape including the letter from Dave Lowe before he made any decision. He agreed and dispatched a clerk to the boat. All this took some time and the impasse continued with the officer sympathetic but standing on his original statement that he really had no authority to interfere. He was trying to end the unwanted stalemate by getting me to agree to submit peacefully for the time being. I stood my ground. I was angry again and ready for a fight. The officer asked his clerk if the High Commissioner was still visiting the island and the clerk said, "Yes, he is with Oscar DeBrum, the District Administer from Majuro." My prospects suddenly brightened when I heard this and I said, "Oscar DeBrum knows me. Will you please ask him to come over here." There was another wait until Peter Coleman, the High Commissioner for the whole Trust Territories entered the room with Oscar DeBrum right behind him. When Oscar walked in, he greeted me warmly and asked what the trouble was. I briefly explained and he turned to Mr.

Coleman and said, "I know this man and his family and can vouch for him. What can we do to help?" Coleman reviewed the whole thing including my papers from the boat and came up with a solution. He said to me, "If you will allow yourself and boat to be anchored temporarily off the island of "Ebye" to satisfy the local authorities, I will get in touch with our attorney general on Siapan and have this arrest thing rescinded. You will not be taken to jail or separated from your family and no one will board your vessel. I think this can be resolved very quickly." I felt relieved and agreed. Oscar shook my hand and said not to worry. With that, I went back to the boat with the sheriff and his men. They untied my lines and I followed them in their small boat to Ebye. We anchored off the main town and they departed. I was disgusted and angry that Jeanne and Susie were so disappointed and had not even been allowed the pleasure of stepping ashore after their hard labor and valiant help in getting our crippled vessel across this last passage. We had a drink, fixed dinner in the quiet anchorage and waited.

Ebye is a small island just a few miles up the atoll from the military facility. It has been labeled "The Slum of the Pacific," perhaps the worse eyesore in the islands. It had hundreds of Micronesians living on it with poor shelter and few conveniences. Even their drinking water had to be brought in by barge. The inhabitants worked at the big base at Kwajalein and were ferried over every morning and back at night. They were not allowed to remain on the main base overnight. There was so much resentment between our government and their authorities, I was frankly fearful of being detained on this island and was thankful that a stroke of luck in meeting Oscar DeBrum had not allowed that to happen.

The next morning, we were sitting on deck after breakfast with a cup of coffee when a small boat approached us at high speed. When they came alongside, I was told I could return to the base and that the problem was resolved. Relieved, we hauled our anchor and made our way back to the main dock at the base. We were boarded by the Harbormaster who knew the whole story by now and he was sympathetic and said to forget it. "Let's get on with repairing your vessel and have you enjoy some rest and relaxation in the process. It sounds like you've earned it."

There was one thing I had to do immediately so I headed for the radio office and sent the following wire:

Pass following message to Dave Lowe, Public Defender from W. A. Corley, Captain, Evening Star. Myself and vessel presently under arrest at Kwajalein as per court order from Judge Brown on Ponape. Your letter on my behalf ignored. Please advise.

The following day, I received an answer.

Pass to W. A. Corley, Master M/V Evening Star. I am in receipt of information on your situation. My letters usually ignored. Please post cash bond on Ponape libel and proceed to Kwajalein for repairs. Please advise me when this is accomplished. I am prepared to proceed further on your behalf. Lowe.

CHAPTER TWENTY-SEVEN

THE ISLAND OF KWAJALEIN was a paradise. It was not very large but within it's confines, there was an airstrip, stores, clubs, outdoor movie theatres, modest homes, schools, office buildings and several thousand civilian workers as well as military personnel. A large company, "Global Associates," had contracted with the government to run the island. They provided all necessary services including a civilian police force. They also ran the shipyard and repair facility from which I now asked for help in repairing my vessel. They readily agreed and, with the big seventy-ton crane at the end of the main dock, lifted "Evening Star" out of the water and blocked her up on the end of the pier. A crowd gathered to take a look at this vessel that a man and his family had sailed leaking and crippled from Ponape and they showered us with friendliness and invitations to their homes. We made some good friends and enjoyed ourselves. The shipyard personnel did most of the work on the boat.

Fred and Nancy Olson were friends of Bob and Patti Arthur on Ponape and helped us in many ways. They both worked for Global and had a daughter a few years' younger than Susie. Katherine and Susie became pals and the Olsons entertained us in their home and showed us around the island and its facilities. We ate out almost every night, either at the clubs or with friends and almost everyone on the island was at the outdoor movies every night for first run films. It was beautiful sitting at the movies in the evening under the stars in the warm tropical air. I couldn't help but remember what this small piece of real estate was like when I first saw it.

In those days, as the Navy R5Ds approached for landing, the island looked not much larger than the airport itself which had a single runway. It was actually a triangular shaped coral motu on the southern end of the atoll. The runway extended the length of the island, ending abruptly at the ocean on both ends. At the approach end, there were all the remains of war. A junk pile of rusting equipment was pushed to the water's edge to get it out of the way. It covered several acres and the sea washed through the skeleton of old trucks, graders, weapons carriers and all manner of other equipment of war. In those days, when our landing roll was completed, we taxied back to the approach end of the runway where there was a low, one-story quonset building that housed the operations office and a crew's mess. Alongside this building was a long, native out-rigger canoe on display. Fifty yards down a path was the first of several more quonset huts that served as crew's quarters. These were just empty floors of bunks where you tried to sleep and escape the mosquitos. These structures were only a hundred yards off the side of the runway and next to the lagoon. A ham radio shack sat on the beach and ran a continual string of phone patches to hams in the states who made telephone connections to families back home. It was a popular place and the only link to the outside world for the men stationed on the island. To them, it was like spending a year in prison and nobody had a kind word for Kwajalein at that time. Farther down the island I vividly remember seeing a wire enclosure with over a hundred Micronesian people, uprooted from their home island of Bikini, so we could test nuclear bombs there.

They were a pitiful, bewildered lot and it was truly a prison to them. The flight crews were always happy to climb on the next arriving flight the following day and, after a twelve hour flight with one stop on tiny Johnston Island, arrive in Hawaii with all it's earthly pleasures. Here I was on this hated island twenty five years later enjoying all the luxuries of home with people who chose to come here for the good salaries and pleasant island living.

As a condition of being able to continue repairs, I had been asked to post a bond of $163.93. This is what I wanted to do before leaving Ponape but was told by my attorney it wasn't necessary. In fact, I wanted the bond to cover all monies owed to the Trust Territory Government for the use of their equipment also. I was in a quandary thinking I was being duly represented by counsel on Ponape, and then finding out that his representation was evidently being totally ignored. What to do? I just wanted the thing cleared up and out of the way but something else bothered me. I had made many friends in these islands and now it appeared I had tried to skip town without paying my bills. This hurt and was not true so I wanted to set the record straight. It seemed I was becoming a victim again. I took a whole day and composed a letter.

Mr. Dave Lowe
Public Defenders Office
June 21, 1976

Dear Dave,

Since you are handling my case against the Trust Territory Government and certain individuals at Ponape, this letter should help to clarify my position and feelings in the matter. I am also writing it for another reason. Because of events in the past two weeks, some of the many friends we have made in these islands may be inclined to believe the skipper of the "Evening Star" left Ponape owing monies to certain individuals and the T.T. Government with no intent of paying lawful debts. To correct these possible assumptions, I intend to give this letter wide circulation among those friends I feel might be interested in the facts.

As you recall, when you agreed to handle my case, I questioned you about the advisability of putting an amount of money equal to all demands in an escrow account or bond. You didn't feel it was necessary and we didn't do so. Instead, you wrote a letter on my behalf stating your office represented me and that we were preparing a case against the T.T. Government and certain individuals. The reason is clearly set forth in the second paragraph of that letter which said:

"The Corley family was ruthlessly victimized by gross nonfeasance by numerous officers and officials of the Trust Territory Government. These actions have resulted in damages in the thousands of dollars and certain irreparable harm to the family and their boat."

In light of this, subsequent actions taken against me this past few days seem irresponsible in the extreme on the part of Ponape officials. Before I get into that and since your office and letter on my behalf seems to be ignored, I propose we take the following action. To clearly show my intent from this point on, I wish to post a bond in whatever legal way you and the court deem proper. This amount of bond should be the total sum of unpaid bills presented to me at Ponape.

To bring you up to date, "Evening Star" obtained a port clearance from Ponape on June 11th and sailed that afternoon at 1530 hours. Just before sailing, Allen Burdick of Micronesia Legal Services came by the boat and said he was representing two men who claimed I owed them $163.93 and asked why I refused to pay them. I explained to him that they were a part of the government crew that stole a great many things and that, as my attorney, you had advised against paying any further billings until we prepared our case. I directed him to your letter of June 8th in Syl Tulley's office for a full explanation of our intent. He asked me if I was sailing and I said yes. He seemed satisfied that the matter was being handled in a reasonable and legal way and departed.

I arrived at Kwajalein about 1000 hours on June 17th and found the people at Global ready and able to repair the boat and the Army agreed to let them do it. My discussions with them were interrupted by the appearance of the local Trust Territory Sheriff who placed both myself and the boat under arrest. He had a court order from Judge Brown at Ponape to hold me and the boat because of the $163.93 bill before mentioned.

This seemed a bit ludicrous to me. They, of course, have every right to establish a lien on the boat but it should have been handled with you. On the other hand, for Judge Brown to have me arrested just reinforces my contention that there is a total disregard for human rights and property on Ponape. I was subsequently held for twenty-four hours without benefit of counsel, bail or any other due process and I still don't know what I am charged with.

Fortunately, the newly appointed High Commissioner, Mr. Peter Coleman, and Oscar DeBrum were on the island and intervened on my behalf with a call to the Attorney General on Siapan with instructions to contact you and resolve this thing. There was nothing they could do to rescind Judge Brown's court order so I was held for the following twenty four hours until the Attorney General could officially intervene. The following morning, I was told by Oscar DeBrum that the matter was settled and that I could take my boat from Ebye and that I was cleared to continue my negotiations for repairs. I agreed to post a bond in the amount of $163.93. I am now back at Kwajalein, boat repairs are under way but no bond papers have yet been drawn for me.

I want this thing resolved, Dave. Please contact me via General Delivery, Kwajalein with instructions how to do it. My plans are to sail for Seattle in about three weeks. Many thanks for your help and I will look forward to hearing from you.

Best regards,

W. A. Corley

With this bit of business out of the way, I concentrated on repairing the boat and enjoying the island and new found friends. Mel Carr was a tug boat skipper who had been on the island for many years and we made his acquaintance soon after arriving. His wife, Ruth, also worked on the island and they had a daughter, Iwalani, who became pals with Susie. Mel graciously gave us the keys to the tug which was tied up only a few feet away from our boat so that we might use the head facilities at night. He and Ruth were both interested in sailing and we became good friends during the few weeks we spent on Kwajalein. They were a great help to us in putting the boat back in some semblance of order and a joy to be with. We knew we had a long ocean voyage ahead of us but for a few weeks, we put it out of our minds and just enjoyed ourselves. After a couple of weeks, I had to tell Jeanne to count me out of any more invitations. I just wasn't getting my work done.

The Global shipyard people did a good job. In a couple of weeks, they had the hull back in good shape and when they were out of the way, I sanded and painted the topsides of the hull with a gleaming coat of white paint. She was beginning to look like her old self again, at least on the outside. We didn't fare quite as well below decks. Some of the locker doors were damaged so badly, they couldn't be repaired and we still had a lot of scars. There was no way to replace our stove so we had to continue with the two one-burner units. I did replace the old battered piece of plywood they were sitting on with a new piece and painted it. The other problem was the engine. We would have had to tear into it to determine the extent of damage, then order parts from the mainland and all that would take a lot of time. I was afraid to get involved with it for fear it would delay our departure indefinitely. It would just have to see us through. Since we could follow the old sailing route out of Kwajalein with the prospect of good winds, I wasn't too concerned.

Although no one even mentioned it again, I was still under the cloud of arrest and unable to leave without that being cleared up. I had not heard anything from Dave Lowe so I wrote him again.

June 26, 1976
Dear Dave,

I has been nine days since I arrived at Kwajalein and was placed under arrest. Since then, I have not heard from you regarding this matter. Are you there, Dave, and if so, may I be informed of what action is being taken on my behalf.

Boat repairs are well under way and I should be able to sail by July 6th. That is about as late as I can safely depart here on a voyage to Seattle because of the short summer season in the North Pacific. I do not intend to sail the boat from Kwajalein unless the vessel is cleared from the court order and arrest. If this is not cleared up by my sailing date, I will climb on an airplane with my family for home and the confiscation of the boat by the Trust Territory government will be complete. I will then seek redress and damages through the U.S. Government and the courts.
Sincerely,
W. A. Corley

I had no intentions of leaving my boat but I hoped this bit of bravado would stir someone to action. I didn't want any delays because of bureaucratic red tape when I was ready to sail. The bond had not been posted and no papers drawn although I had inquired at the Trust Territory Liaison office several times. Finally on July 3rd, I received a letter from Dave Lowe.

July 1, 1976
W. A. Corley
c/o General Delivery, Kwajalein Island
Dear Bill,

I am sorry that there has been a great deal of confusion in this matter. I just received your letter of June 29, 1976. In that I only received it thirty minutes ago, I deemed this to be the immediate reply to which you are entitled. However, let me assure you that some of the facts are not as you have them and it may be due to communications difficulties here and it may be due to something else, I am not sure.

First, I did, in fact, send a copy of the letter I wrote on your behalf to the Public Works Director, Ponape. I do not know why it was not received but upon my return to Ponape on Wednesday, June 16, 1976, I caused another copy to be hand delivered to Mr. Tulley. Then, I proceeded to Siapan on Friday, June 19, 1976. When I arrived at the airport, I learned that you had been served with libel and arrest for yourself and the vessel. I immediately attempted to contact Kwajalein and was successful on Monday, June 21, 1976, in contacting Mr. Murph Ownby of the Trust Territory with a phone message for you. It was that you were to deposit bail on the warrant and proceed to Kwajalein for repairs. I also informed Mr. Ownby that he should have you telephone me here as soon as you arrived Kwajalein and he assured me that you would do so if there were any problems. I then received a dispatch, copy enclosed, concerning your status. I then proceeded to immediately return that dispatch to you with instructions as to what you should do. A copy of that dispatch is also enclosed for your information.

159

I am truly sorry about the communications delay and the fact that these circumstances occurred when I was already in the process of moving my principal office to Majuro but was going to Siapan for a summer of necessary work. If I do not hear from you, I will assume you received this letter. Follow the instructions and I will contact you in the near future.
Very Truly Yours,
David Lowe

I read this letter and the dispatches, trying to understand what it was telling me. Then I filed it and went back to work. Maybe my second letter, which would have crossed in the mail, would bring better results. By this time, I had no hope of accomplishing anything further. I just wanted to post a bond in whatever amount they wanted, forget about it and get clearance to leave. That clearance was forthcoming on July 6th, the deadline I had set forth in my last letter.

Mr. Ownby, the Trust Territory Liaison Officer, asked me over to his office and handed me a paper.

6 July 76
Mr. Corley
Owner, vessel Evening Star.

In accordance with high court order dated July 6, 1976 and signed by Judge Brown, associate justice of the Trust Territory of the Pacific Islands concerning civil actions #39-76 and 40-76 and in compliance with order and release from custody, this is to state that W. M Ownby Trust Territory Liaison Officer, Kwajalein, Marshall Islands is in receipt of a cashiers check made payable to the clerk of courts, Ponape in the amount of Fifteen Hundred Dollars as required by the attached document.

Having complied with the attached, the vessel "Evening Star" her tackle, etc., shall be released from custody and all restraints therefrom, and is free to travel outside of the Trust Territory.

I handed over the check and mentally wrote it off. I was free to sail and would be ready within a few days to do just that. In retrospect, I should have known better than to try to pursue a legal remedy in this vast complicated structure of local government and U. S. control. With poor communications everyone had probably done the best they could. I ultimately blamed myself for being such a damn fool and creating the problem by putting the boat on the reef in the first place.

Evening Star at Kwajalein for repairs

CHAPTER TWENTY-EIGHT

T HE HULL REPAIRS WERE FINISHED and after a final coat of paint on her topsides, the big crane lowered "Evening Star" off the dock and back into her element. They gave us a nice berth alongside the main dock in protected water and we were ready for final preparations to sail. The big squarsail yard had been lying alongside the wharf for painting and we hoisted it aloft again and secured it to the mainmast. I set a date for sailing only four days away. With the engine doubtful, I had plotted a course to Seattle staying well into the sailing ship route and it looked like roughly a six-thousand-mile trip. That meant a possible forty-day voyage for which we had to provision and prepare. Normally, facing such a long sail would have been somewhat distressing to us but we were going home and that made all the difference. For the first time in months, we were having fun again and with a light step and happy hearts, we threw ourselves into the last few days of work preparing our little ship for sea.

Mel Carr was a great help. He was a frustrated sailor who couldn't get away himself for an adventure like ours so I think he enjoyed helping us put the ship in order. He helped me get the rigging back in shape and somehow found the necessary equipment and supplies needed. After many trips to the food stores and a couple of hard days stowing everything aboard, we were almost ready to go. One problem we faced was our lack of any kind of jackets for the cold weather we might encounter as we moved back into northern waters. In this part of the world, a coat of any kind was just something you never thought about and was actually hard to come by. Mel solved that one by thinking of the only place on the island where a coat was actually needed, that being the large cold storage plant where ice and perishables were stored. He talked the supply officer in charge into selling us a couple of heavy Navy flight deck jackets and they threw in another used one with the word "reefer" emblazoned across the back. This became Susie's and you could always pick her out of the crowd with such a distinctive piece of clothing. She earned the nickname, "Reefer."

On Saturday afternoon, Mel and I were working on deck when Susie and his daughter, Iwalani, came aboard and approached me.

"Dad, can we talk to you a minute?" I said "sure" and they laughingly laid it on us. "Dad, Iwalani would like to make the trip home with us. She is out of school for the summer and could be back before it starts again. It would be so nice for me if she could go." I don't know which of us was more surprised, Mel or myself, but I said, "sure Honey, it's OK with me but I'm sure her mother and father would have something to say about it." To my great surprise, Both Mel and Ruth agreed that afternoon to let Iwalani go with us and as we were leaving the following morning, they had lots to do in a hurry to prepare her for the trip. Jeanne took another look at our food supply to be sure we would be covered with another mouth to feed. At a final dinner that evening at the Carr's, there were two very excited young ladies and, I suppose, if the truth were known, two somewhat apprehensive parents.

On a quiet Sunday morning, the 10th of July, we prepared to leave. Mel and Ruth were to accompany us the first forty miles to "Roi" Island on the northern end of the atoll. We would spend the night there at anchor and they would fly back on a local flight the following morning. Just before leaving, Ruth called me aside and thrust a large package in my hand. We had talked about the fact that all three of the girls would have a birthday at sea before we reached Seattle and she had prepared a package for each of them that included a small gift and bottle of wine. She asked that I hide the package so it would be a surprise and I agreed. What a nice gesture, but then, this was one fine woman. Mel also had a going away gift for the boat. It was a beautiful handheld wooden fishing line holder that contained a couple-of-hundred feet of heavy hand line and jig. That piece of equipment has provided many a fish dinner over the years and is still aboard to this day.

With a moderate tradewind blowing, we had a fine and festive sail up the atoll in the protected waters of the lagoon. Then, a great barbecue steak dinner and a last night in a quiet anchorage. In the morning, there were a lot of good-byes and a few tears before Mel and Ruth departed and we watched as their plane took off and disappeared heading south. We had some time before a favorable tide would help us through the pass in the reef so we hauled water to top our tanks before leaving the anchorage about noon. It was a short run to the entrance of the closest break in the reef and under full sail, we jibed through the pass and headed north on a beam reach into the northeast trades. After two-and-a-half years at sea, with many changes of fortune, we were headed home.

Within two hours, Kwajalein Atoll disappeared below the horizon as quickly as it had appeared for us only a few weeks before. The trades were blowing fresh and we sailed north with a clean, freshly-painted bottom at hull speed. Sinbad, the cat, was sick for the first few hours but quickly recovered as he always did but with Iwalani, it was a different story. She became sick soon after we reached the open sea and remained so. We all felt sorry for her but could do no more than try to make her comfortable and wait for it to pass. The following morning, we had the island of "Rongerik" off our port bow and passed it at mid morning only a few miles off our beam. Poor Iwalani was still very sick with "Mal de Mer" and begged me to put her ashore, her adventurous spirit now totally gone. I could see the desperation and hate in her eyes when I refused to consider it. I assured her she was not the first to have to go through this initiation of seamanship and that it would pass. (Try telling this to someone who thinks she may be sick like this for the whole voyage.)

As I stood the long night watch that evening, I had time to ponder the events of the past few months and search for a reason why some of the people of the Trust Territory had treated us so shabbily. Maybe the answer partially rested with the people of the island we had just sailed by. When the whole population of "Bikini" was uprooted from their ancestral home island in 1946 so we could test our atomic bomb, they were dumped on "Rongerick" Atoll to make a new life as best they could. There were only a hundred-and-sixty-seven people but it was a whole nation to them. Each island poses different problems of survival for its inhabitants. They must learn from trial and error what they can and cannot grow and how to fish the local waters. What fish are edible and which ones are deadly poisonous. After a year of nearly becoming destitute, their plight was recognized by the Navy and they were moved to Kwajalein. That's where I first saw them in a pitiful state behind a wire enclosure when I flew through as a Navy man after the war. They were later shipped to "Kili" Island in the extreme southern end of the Marshall Islands. This island was not even an atoll and they had to adjust again. A United Nation's mission investigated "Kili" in 1956 and reported:

> Bikini, with an extensive lagoon, had afforded it's people the opportunity of making use of an abundance of fish and good anchorage for boats. Kili does not possess

either. Bikini has a larger land area than Kili with heavier rainfall and richer soil. When the people of Bikini were moved to Kili, they had to learn new methods of cultivating the soil and food plants that did not exist on Bikini. The lack of a protected anchorage, the unfavorable axis of the island with relation to the prevailing tradewinds, and the narrow shelving reef cause the island to be isolated during many months of the year. Landing conditions are possible only during brief periods between November and late March. The unfavorable surf conditions prevent them from fishing a lot of the time and the loading of copra and the landing of merchandise for local consumption was impossible during a large part of the year.

I had read that one of the ships that put into Kili with supplies for a starving population was wrecked on the reef and that another ship that took it's place was severely damaged. In 1947, the whole population of "Eniwetok" suffered a similar fate when they were also uprooted and shipped to the island of "Ujelang" to start a new life. Much later in 1954, our testing of the Hydrogen bomb got out of control and radioactive fallout fell on the island population of both "Uterik" and "Ronglap." One hundred-and-fifty-four people from "Uterik" and eighty-two from "Rongelap" were moved to Majuro for observation and treatment. The people of Uterik were away for a year before being allowed to return home while the whole population of Rongelap was kept in exile on Majuro for three years before being allowed to return to their own atoll. All these people suffered from radiation sickness, loss of hair, skin lesions and weeping ulcers. How this experience will effect their descendants may not be determined for generations to come.

As we travelled through these islands, it became apparent that our policy toward these people under the Trusteeship had been a disaster. Instead of giving them the help they needed in education and building a solid economy, we had just made a welfare state out of the whole Trust Territory. Consequently, the Islanders had lost their heritage and their hope. When we first took over these islands after the war, the local people were not far removed from the subsistence economy they had lived under for centuries. They welcomed the largess that was thrust upon them by our government but the new generation is much better educated and knowledgable of what is happening in the world. They are outraged at the U. S. Government for what we did to the Marshallese people and feel there is no moral justification for destroying their way of life just to maintain a strategic power base in the Pacific. As I finished the last of the thermos of coffee and waited to be relieved, I could sum up my own feelings: I wasn't happy about some of the treatment I had received in my time of misfortune, but deep down, I could understand the anger and frustration of the people.

In four days of running due north, we made good time in the northeast trades, covering almost six hundred miles. Iwalani had recovered by the third day and everybody had settled down to a sea routine. Jeanne cooked those wonderful meals she was so capable of on our little one burner stoves and Susie and Iwalani played the guitar and generally enjoyed each other's company. For Susie to have a companion at sea was gratifying to me, especially on such a long voyage. Sinbad chased the flying fish as they hit the deck in the evening hours and we all read a lot. We passed Wake island, fifty miles to leeward and continued on our northerly course. On July 25th, the first of those surprise packages came out as we celebrated Iwalani's 16th birthday. Jeanne made a cake and we even had candles. Ruth's package, of course, was the high point of the evening as it was such a total surprise. After ten days, we reached thirty degrees north latitude and the northern limits of the northeast tradewinds. The weather became unsettled and our progress slowed as we moved into the area known as the horse latitudes. This is the area between the two wind systems, the Trades and the Westerlys. We needed to gain more northing to put us into the westerlies which would take us east to our destination. When the wind fell light, I turned on the engine to charge our batteries and keep us moving. It didn't have much power and would only idle along.

We changed course to northeast and sailed in changing wind conditions for the next few days trying to gain more northing. One day, we only made forty miles for the twenty four hour run and on another, we sailed fifty miles but in the wrong direction because of contrary winds. It was slow going as we fought our way north to better winds but we made some headway and crossed the International Date Line on the 27th. Then we had a few days of pretty good runs and found ourselves at forty five degrees north latitude where we should have had plenty of favorable winds but didn't. We were becalmed in light airs and I called on the engine for the last time. It temporarily responded with a belch of black smoke and then quit for good. We rolled around for the next twenty-four hours with occasional light winds, giving us only a twenty-mile run. Crew morale deteriorated badly and we had the first mishap of the voyage. Trying to cook with the increased rolling of the boat in heavy swells, Jeanne burned herself badly on the arm. She was depressed and Iwalani became sick again. On top of everything else, one of our little stoves became disabled leaving us with only one burner to cook on. Things changed for the better though when the wind finally came up steady out of the west. We raised the big squaresail and laid a course direct to Seattle for the first time.

On August 5th, we celebrated Jeanne's birthday. Susie and Iwalani took over the galley for the whole day and gave her a respite. She was in better spirits now and smiled frequently, watching and listening to the two girls struggle to bake a cake and prepare dinner on the one burner. It was an all day affair and, of course, we had a great dinner with cake, birthday toasts and another gift package with wine, compliments of Ruth Carr. We had been at sea almost a month now and an event such as this was a welcome change of routine and a great lift to the spirits of the crew.

For the next nine days it was mostly overcast but the winds held steady and we moved eastward at a good pace. Those jackets we had managed to acquire on Kwajalein came in handy, especially on the night watches. We were now only five hundred miles west of Cape Flattery and our landfall when the winds again fell light and our progress stalled. For one whole day, we drifted on a calm sea without making any headway on our course. With no engine, all we could do was wait. It was a good time to celebrate another birthday and we did, Susie's 15th. By this time, there was no surprise in Ruth's gift. Susie knew she wouldn't be left out and enjoyed her little present as much as the others had. Another incident broke the monotony the following day. Sinbad was playing on the bow and suddenly fell overboard. Jeanne was at the helm, saw him take the dive and reacted quickly. She grabbed the big fish net that was fortunately lying on top of the aft cabin and scooped him out of the water as he passed the aft end of the boat. It was a close call because, without an engine, he would have been impossible to find and get back aboard.

The wind came back after twenty four hours and we were underway again, everybody watching that line move over the chart toward our destination only a few hundred miles away. A long voyage becomes tolerable when you approach the end of it and the excitement begins to build in anticipation of a landfall. Because of the overcast, I hadn't had a good position in two days and was running on a dead reckoning course. On the morning of August 20th, we searched the horizon for land and before noon, the high mountains of Vancouver Island appeared in the distance. I was able to get a shot of the sun and establish our position which put us off Barkley Sound, a little north of the entrance to the Strait Of Juan De Fuca. It was a beautiful afternoon with light winds and none of us could take our eyes off those beautiful green mountains as we slowly moved down the coast. The winds fell to almost nothing that evening and we were frustrated to be so close and stalled again. We drifted with the current all night and into the next day before the wind finally freshened and we put up every bit of sail we could carry and entered the wide mouth of the Strait. We had ninety miles to go before reaching Seattle and feeling solid land under our feet again. By the middle of the afternoon, we were running hard down the Strait when another vessel hove into view coming from the opposite direction. It was some distance off but looked familiar as I viewed it through the binoculars. As it came abeam, it changed course to intercept us and for over an hour, we slowly converged. I couldn't imagine why it was interested in us until it finally came alongside and turned out to be "Nunaga," the boat owned by Pete Francis. We had last seen them in Tahiti over a year ago. He hailed us and yelled, "I knew that was you. There's not another boat in the Pacific that looks like "Evening Star" with that squaresail flying. What a small world!" He bore off on his original course and we continued on for home, hoping to arrive the next afternoon. It was not to be. The winds died with the sun and we drifted with the current through the night and well into the next morning. Finally, under way again, we only made it as far as Dungeness Point before being becalmed for another night. It was frustrating being so close and unable to get those last few miles under our keel. This was the way it was for all sailors before engines came into general use. After forty two days at sea and a long time since fresh food had appeared on our table, we could almost smell the hamburgers and fresh lettuce ashore.

On August 24th, I timed the tide right to help us through Admiralty Inlet and with both the favorable tide and a nice breeze, we boiled through the inlet and into Puget Sound. We were now only thirty miles from Seattle and my plan was to go into Shilshole Bay but halfway down the sound, the wind died to almost nothing again. Faced with having to spend another night before landing, I bore off for Kingston at a snail's pace.

170

We had all sail up but were moving so slowly, I launched our hard dinghy with the outboard engine and motored around the boat taking pictures. Late in the afternoon we sailed and drifted to within a couple of hundred yards of the ferry dock at Kingston. In desperation, I took our vessel under tow with the dinghy and rounded the breakwater. We tied up to an end dock that was empty and after forty three days out of Kwajalein, four of us and one cat stepped ashore.

EPILOGUE

OUR ODYSSEY WAS COMPLETE. Remember Webster's defini-
tion of odyssey: "A long wandering marked usually by
many changes of fortune." So it had been for us.

A few days after we arrived in Kingston, Iwalani, a much
more mature and experienced young woman, was on a plane
headed back to her family and island home. She was received
on Kwajalein as a young heroine and recounted her experiences for the local newspaper.

Susie returned to Southern California within a few weeks to
live with her mother and re-enter school for the fall semester. I
was very proud of her and could only pay her my greatest
tribute. She had been an able shipmate. Today, she is the wife
of an attorney and has two children.

Jeanne's father was very ill and she was soon on a plane for
Texas to visit and help care for him. My admiration and respect
for this woman is unbounded. We have since gone our separate
ways but my feelings have not changed. This book is dedicated
to her.

I returned to work at my former company and was immediately sent to Colorado for an extended period of time to work on

some problems there. I worked for over a year before retiring again. I could not handle the corporate existence anymore.

Sinbad, the cat, continued to live aboard the boat in Shilshole Bay until several months after we returned, I found him dead on the street one morning, the victim of an automobile. I was on my way to work for an important meeting when I discovered him under a bush by the side of the street. I forgot the meeting and returned to the boat and changed from my suit to some old clothes. Then, with a small pick ax, I buried him on the hill above the marina by the railroad tracks and returned to the boat to make an entry in the ship's log. "Sinbad died this morning. He was a fine little shipmate and we will miss him."

The storm that was forming close to Ponape as we struggled to get the boat off the reef in those final days became hurricane "Billie" and smashed into the Marianias Islands causing great damage.

A couple of months after we returned, I received a disposition from the court on Ponape awarding the $1500.00 dollar bond to my creditors.

"Evening Star" gradually shed her scars and was put back into shape below decks. She's a proud old girl who has carried this writer many thousands of miles since.

"Paradise"—Well, it is full of bugs—problems—incredible beauty—adventure—and it still exists today in the hearts of dreamers as the Valhalla of the human experience.

COLOPHON
A NOTE ON THE TYPE
IN WHICH THIS BOOK IS SET

THIS BOOK IS SET IN CASLON 540, a modern adaptation of a type designed by the first William Caslon (1692-1766). The Caslon face has had two centuries of ever-increasing popularity in the United States—it is of interest to note that the first copies of the Declaration of Independence and the first paper currency distributed to the citizens of the new-born nation were printed in this type face.

The text of this book was composed by Linda Maxwell. The cover was created by Lito Castro. Art Direction by John Mello. Printed and bound by Blue Dolphin Press in the United States of America.